PICKING WILLOWS

PICKING WILLOWS

WITH DAISY AND LILLY BAKER, MAIDU BASKET MAKERS OF LAKE ALMANOR

PAT LINDGREN-KURTZ

iUniverse, Inc.
Bloomington

Picking Willows
With Daisy and Lilly Baker, Maidu Basket Makers of Lake Almanor

iUniverse books may be ordered through booksellers or by contacting:

iUniverse
1663 Liberty Drive
Bloomington, IN 47403
www.iuniverse.com
1-800-Authors (1-800-288-4677)

ISBN: 978-1-4620-5551-7 (sc)
ISBN: 978-1-4620-5552-4 (e)

Printed in the United States of America

iUniverse rev. date: 09/27/2011

These heartfelt writings are dedicated to:

My husband, Cornell, who cherished our day-by-day living and invited
Daisy and Lilly into our world and happily shared theirs,
Our daughter, Kit, who embraced and loved these two women as family
members for five decades and accepted Daisy as a third grandmother,
And to my parents, other family members, and many friends who
enriched these journeys with their unabashed joy.

Words of Praise

Pat's tone and sensitivity with regard to the situation in which the Mountain Maidu found themselves is very much ahead of its time and clearly a reflection of her respect for and experience with Daisy and Lilly Baker. *Terri Castaneda, PhD, Associate Professor and Museum Director, Department of Anthropology, California State University, Sacramento.*

This book is vivid and well written, a charming basket of untold California history, family memoir, and especially friendships among talented artists from two different cultures. Pick up *Picking Willows* and weave yourself a rich reading experience. *Bruce Shelly, Screenwriter and Author.*

Picking Willows is an important story of art and culture, one that only artist Pat Kurtz could tell because of her unique five-decade friendship with Mountain Maidu basket makers Daisy and Lilly Baker. Kurtz's memoir is loaded with valuable historical information and interesting stories about these native basket makers and the difficulties they experienced living in Western society while trying to keep their cultural traditions alive. *Tom Peek, Writer and Writing Teacher.*

"Picking willows?" questioned my friend Gail Tousey. "I know about picking flowers. Tell me about picking willows."

Contents

Front Cover – Lilly Baker, Kit Kurtz, and Daisy Baker strip leaves from willow rods at Lake Almanor, California – 1957.

PREFACE

The seed of a cross-cultural friendship was sowed in 1955 when my family first met Lilly Baker and her mother, Daisy. Our friendship grew, and we developed an unquestioning acceptance of each other. Throughout the years, we shared an inclusive and sincere belief that we were one family and there was no question about it—we liked each other. Contrasts in our cultural backgrounds only enriched our experiences. Daisy and Lilly were indigenous Mountain Maidu weavers who came from a large family of basket makers. We were the newcomers, living on lands that had once belonged to the Mountain Maidu.

How did this happen? Perhaps I have felt an appreciation to all Maidu—then and now—because, during the gold-rush era, a Maidu family saved the life of Wilhelm Georg Adolph von Breyman, my grandfather. In the 1870s, my grandfather advertised his services throughout the area—as an itinerant large animal doctor in the Woodland, California, newspapers and as a vendor of portable gates and fences in Sacramento's paper, the *Daily Bee*. My mother told us that on a journey to visit one of his customers in the foothills northeast of Sacramento; my grandfather became deathly ill and lost his way. A Maidu family found him and carried him into their round house where they healed him by sweating the illness from him. This was particularly remarkable because tension was high between the Indians and pioneers at that time, and my grandfather was always grateful for the Maidu family's care.

Daisy and Lilly Baker practiced their cultural traditions, including the making of baskets, which were so important in basic Maidu life. Baskets made by the California Maidu have been recognized as some of the finest made by any North American tribe. These beautiful twined, coiled, and wicker baskets were essential containers for the harvesting, preparing, cooking, and storing of foods. Baskets of the finest craftsmanship were made for show, trade, or gifts. Some were burned as offerings honoring the dead in annual traditional rites.

Willow shoots of varying sizes were the primary fibers in Maidu basket construction. The first important step in basket making was "picking willows," as Daisy and Lilly called the gathering of the young shoots of the native gray willow. Willows, the warp and the core foundation, provided structural strength to the baskets. Each stitch and twist of the other fibers bound them together, adding texture, design, and beauty to the basket. It was during these willow-picking excursions that our lifelong relationship with Daisy and Lilly Baker began.

During our five decades of friendship, their life stories unfolded. Daisy Baker, born around 1879, shared glimpses of her life from the late nineteenth century into the twentieth century. She was thought to have been eighty-five years old when she died in January 1964. Born in 1911, Lilly passed on at the age of ninety-five in November 2006 and the picking of willows for traditional Maidu basket making ceased.

Woven together in this story are Daisy's and Lilly's recollections of early Maidu life, pioneer impositions, and a record of industrial changes to their environment. They tried to cling to familiar, century-old traditions that allowed them to survive off the land. In spite of discrimination and life-threatening events, these women continued to pick willows and make their baskets. And for over a half century, a quiet inner drive encouraged Daisy and Lilly to share their traditions by giving talks and demonstrations to hundreds of schoolchildren and an untold number of diverse audiences at community gatherings, art shows, and civic events.

As a watercolor artist and an arts-and-crafts teacher, I naturally became fascinated with Daisy's and Lilly's basket making. The time-consuming gathering and preparing of native materials for the eventual weaving of various types of containers amazed me. Realizing a need to record and recognize these creative people, I immersed myself in a study of the Maidu culture in graduate school and published my master's thesis on the history of the area, which included Daisy's and Lilly's pioneering experiences.

When reminiscing through decades of family events, I see how our mutual experiences were woven together in many amazing ways. The sense of awe embraces me for having had this rare privilege of inclusion especially with their unabashed sharing of past history and basket making activities. This is my story of Daisy and Lilly Baker, whom I grew to know and love.

INTRODUCTION

On a hot August afternoon in 1947, I drove between steep rocky canyon walls, following the Feather River into California's northeastern Sierra to Indian Valley in Plumas County. Pine-forested, towering, and rugged mountains embraced the small valley, and cool breezes welcomed me. I had grudgingly applied for a job teaching art in a small high school. I didn't want to be a teacher. Fresh out of college as an art major, I had been unable to find a position using my artistic talents in San Francisco. Upon the persuasion of my eldest brother, a counselor with the Veterans Administration, I eventually applied for a job through the University of California Teacher Placement Office in Berkeley and immediately received five job offers. The highest salary, three thousand dollars per year from the Greenville School District in Indian Valley, caught my attention. If I took that offer, I could save a lot of money and return to a city life in San Francisco within a couple of years.

On that August day, the enchanting view assured me that I had been led to the right place to begin my working career. Indian Valley reminded me of Estes Park, Colorado, where I had learned to ski earlier in the year. Being a romantic with a spirit of adventure, I knew that if I taught school in Indian Valley, I could ski all through the winter. I accepted the job, and the teaching staff kindly provided me with in-house training during that first year.

The gold-rush pioneers were so impressed by the great number of Maidu Indians living in this mountain valley that they naturally named it Indian Valley. The student body at the Greenville Junior Senior High School included children from the families of the Maidu Indians, pioneer merchants, loggers, lumbermen, miners, ranchers, and dust-bowl escapees from Oklahoma. With extraordinary hunting and fishing opportunities, some families lived entirely off the land. Learning to teach became challenging, as I naively believed that all children came from families where the parents held education in high esteem—as in my own family—and the children were yearning to learn and be taught. I had great expectancy for their success, and I made a sincere effort to treat all students with equal fairness and respect. Soon it became apparent that my values of equal respect for all were being tested, and I had my first experiences with discrimination. Race and lifestyle were the measuring stick for giving respect for many in the community.

In June 1948, I married Cornell Kurtz from Ohio. He loved the mountains as much as I did, and he received a position teaching the sixth grade in the Greenville Elementary School. Adventures and challenges tested us with varying disguises during that first year of marriage. Severe weather arrived with a record snowfall in December, introducing the coldest winter of the century. Temperatures stayed below zero for twenty days in January 1949. Our water and plumbing froze for three months, requiring us to bathe and wash in friends' homes. The high school shop teacher, George Benton, saved us by offering us a small cabin on his silver-fox farm deep in the forests on the west side of Lake Almanor, twenty miles from Greenville. It was a cozy cabin with water flowing from a mountain spring, a small wood cook-stove, a fireplace, a huge woodshed, and no phone. Still three feet deep in frozen snow, we had to wait for a full snowmelt before moving in. Though very small and simple in decor, we called it our honeymoon cottage. Three years later, on January 10, 1952, we had an unexpected and record-breaking snowfall. Snow fell without ceasing for several days, burying the cabin under ten feet of light and fluffy snow. It marooned us for two weeks before the county snowplows opened our road and rescued us. I was pregnant, and we were expecting our child in March.

It was time to move and build our own home. In 1951, we bought land on the east shore of Lake Almanor. It was located in a small meadow with a grand view of Mount Lassen across the lake. Less snow fell there, and people dubbed the area "the banana belt." We lived on that beautiful location for over fifty years. Early on, I discovered that I had been unaware of Cornell's secret dream—which had been deeply influenced by Thoreau's *Walden*. As a city boy from Toledo, he wanted to live off the land and lead a simple life. As an island girl born in Hawaii, my wish was to live in the big city of San Francisco. But my wish was an opposite desire, and it quickly dissolved as we became pioneers involved with the building of our first home.

1. Our view of Mount Lassen from Lake Almanor's east shore, 1950.
Eastman Kodak Store, Susanville, CA.

1

An Unexpected Adventure Begins

As we built that first home in 1952, little did we realize that an unexpected cultural adventure lay before us. The home-site was bordered by deep forests of pine, fir, and cedar. Fallen split-rail fences enclosed part of the land overgrown with willows and alders. A creek, teeming with brook trout, bordered the eastern boundary and continued across the north portion, providing water for irrigation ditches that traversed the land.

When we planned to move to that small meadow to build our home, we hoped that a spring might provide a domestic water supply for us. Numerous springs formed small creeks along the east shore. Cornell selected a wet spot near the home-site, and, with only a shovel, he dug a large hole. As his digging progressed, clear water bubbled up through the clay-like mud. A viable spring flowed forth for our water supply. By excavating the hole over six feet deep and six feet square, and lining the sides with concrete walls, he built a reservoir that filled quickly with clean, sparkling water from an underground source.

One day, a large man, Indian Henry, the father of two of my husband's students, walked onto our property and asked for permission to drink from the spring. Cornell proudly led him to his new reservoir, and Indian Henry abruptly said, "No!" He headed into a nearby willow thicket and pushed aside accumulated layers of fallen and broken branches.

With some difficulty and much curiosity, we followed him through the brambles to the end of an obscure and short trail. In the cool shade, under a canopy of branches, lay a sparkling jewel: a moss-edged, rock-lined pool overflowing with crystal clear water. We were awed by its hidden beauty. It beckoned to us. Along with Indian Henry, we dropped to our knees and took a cool, refreshing drink with cupped hands. We reverently named it "The Indian Spring."

To begin construction on our house, Cornell built a garage to serve as our temporary housing. We felt like pioneers with no close neighbors, phone, or mail service. After a day's work, we bathed in the lake. We thoroughly enjoyed exploring the lakeshore. Although it was strewn with eyesore piles of driftwood, being a man-made lake, the water level lowered during the summer months, and the wave action exposed many artifacts: still-intact arrowheads, scraping tools of obsidian, basalt, jasper, and chert, and grinding implements of basalt. These objects told us that the early residents were hunters, fishermen, and gatherers. They chipped the native rocks and minerals to form their fine tools. As we gradually began to landscape around our dwelling, we periodically unearthed grinding rocks and arrowheads. It became obvious that our home-site had once been an Indian camp.

Before we moved from the fox farm cabin on the west side of the lake, George Benton, our landlord, shared his treasure trove of stories about the development of the lake. He told us how Great Western Power Company had built an earthen dam to flood Big Meadows and, in 1914, created Lake Almanor for hydroelectric power. He knew our future neighbors, the Maidu Indians, who lived on and used the remaining meadowlands along the east shore before developers bought and subdivided them in 1949. Still living there was a very smart and wise Indian, Ole Salem. George told us that before the turn of the century, Ole received his Indian allotment of 160 acres from the federal government as required under the Dawes Act of 1887. He exchanged his forested land with nearby Westwood's prosperous Red River Lumber Company for arable land bordering the east side of Big Meadows. Ole developed the land and planted orchards, grew raspberries, and raised cattle, along with several draft horses. Late in the nineteenth century, Ole married, and his wife gave him his first son, Carl. The first wife died, and Ole married her sister, who bore him a second son. The second wife died, and as required by Maidu tradition, he married the third and last sister. A third son was born, and the third wife died. His fourth wife was Rosie Meadows, Daisy Baker's sister and Lilly's aunt. Gradually a small family community grew on Ole's land.

Our first meeting with our Maidu neighbors occurred in the early fall of 1954. One afternoon, there was a knock on our door. A handsome Indian man introduced himself as Carl Salem. He asked for our permission to mow the meadow grasses between our house and the lake. He needed hay for winter bedding and fodder for his livestock. We agreed that mowing the drying grasses was a good idea.

Several days later, Carl's brother Roy and two cousins, Bill and Rollin Baker, arrived early in the morning with a horse-drawn wagon loaded with mowing equipment. Carl followed in his pink Chrysler sedan adorned with sweeping rear fins; his stepmother, Rosie Salem, was in the front seat. He drove down the driveway and parked in the upper meadow so that Rosie could watch the harvesting activity. Two men quickly harnessed two draft horses to a large mower and began cutting the grass. The other men followed with pitchforks and rakes, arranging the freshly mowed hay into rows. Statue-like, Rosie watched from the car with arms folded across her chest. When the cut hay was raked, pitched, and piled high onto the wagon, the horses were unhitched from the mower and harnessed to the wagon. Two men then hee-hawed their load up onto the highway and headed to the Salem ranch about a mile down the road. This process was repeated until all of the grasses were cut and hauled away. Carl appeared pleased with the abundance of the harvest. We hardly realized that we were witnessing a unique scene in a fast-closing era, and horse-drawn farm equipment would soon become obsolete.

2

Our Early Years with Daisy and Lilly Baker

Meeting Daisy and Lilly

One day in 1955 I received a request to appear for jury duty in Quincy, our county seat, which was seventy miles away. I had to find a babysitter for our preschool-aged daughter, Kit. Told that Lilly Baker worked as a housekeeper and nanny for families living by the lake, I drove to the Salem ranch where she lived in a small cabin with her mother and two brothers, Rollin and Bill. From the east shore highway, I followed a gravel road along fenced meadowlands. Grazing workhorses lifted their heads and eyed me passing by. Approaching a large arbor of trellised raspberries next to a flowering apple orchard, I saw the first of several buildings, the gray and weatherworn Baker cabin. A small creek edged with yellow monkey flowers and forget-me-nots trickled past the front steps. On a small front porch, a black-and-white dog sat on a worn sofa. He growled at me. I stayed in the car. An older woman stood quietly in the shadowed corner of the porch, while a young Indian lady wearing jeans and white shirt came out of the house and politely greeted me. It was Lilly. She agreed to help me and care for Kit but added that she did not drive and needed a ride.

Bringing her to our home on that first day, Lilly came alone. I think I had to meet with her approval to see if she wanted to work for me, because her mother, Daisy, decided to come with Lilly the next day and thereafter. Their smiles, quiet openness, and innocent trust won us over.

Lilly was slender and about five feet five inches tall. She was considerably taller than her mother. Dressed in jeans and a plaid shirt, her long black hair was pulled away from a full and smiling face. Her eyes shone brightly. She giggled and laughed often and expressed a keen sense of humor. She loved animals. We were told that she had been quite a horsewoman in her youth. She talked about enjoying the Appaloosa horse shows and races at the county fairs. Our cat and dog felt her tender sense of care and immediately followed her everywhere.

Daisy Meadows Baker appeared humble and reticent. Naturally unassuming, she quietly observed life unfolding around her. She was around five feet tall. Her straight, gray hair was drawn back and twisted into a knot at the back of her head. Daisy's eyes sparkled and her warm smile appeared welcoming in spite of the heavy wrinkles lining her face. A well-used apron covered a calico dress that reached to her ankles above dark cotton hose and heavily worn shoes. Reading wasn't her strength, but she certainly could count.

Daisy and Kit teamed up, quickly becoming buddies, and they would tease Lilly. They picked willows and walked along the beach discovering "things" together. In middle school, Kit recalled their walks in a poem:

> I am five maybe -- Maybe not quite that
> Maybe more
> Memories never seem quite governed by years to me.
> Daisy isn't governed by years either.
>
> Lilly and her mother Daisy come to my house.
> I have been to theirs, too.
> Their house is different to me, dark inside,
> and smelled of people living.
> Lilly and Daisy come sometimes to take care of me.
> Really Daisy and I take care of Lilly.
> One time Daisy and I taught Lilly to count.
> I will tell you of that.

Daisy knows how to count because
She is old and Maidu Indian.
She knows how to count the geese going south
and coming north again.
And the first snowflakes.
And the fine stitches she makes with fern root
that makes patterns in her baskets.

I know how to count because I just learned.
And maybe even though I am blonde
Because Daisy teaches me Indian things.

Lilly can't count
Even though she is Maidu Indian, too.
She doesn't get the same answer
As Daisy and I do, so Daisy and I agree
Lilly can't count.

Of course, they knew Lilly really could count. The three of them happily played games. Lilly, Daisy, and Kit "became family." They called Kit their blonde Indian. While Lilly cleaned our house, Kit and Daisy took their walks along the beach. Geese, ducks, and other waterfowl flocked on the water. Seagulls scolded in the sky above. Kit and Daisy searched for arrowheads below a rock outcropping, while excited woodchucks whistled at them. Evidently, the Maidu had chipped their arrow points and scrapers while sitting on those boulders. Daisy's sharp eyes discovered a beautifully sculptured shaman's pipe nestled in the washed gravels.

Daisy told Kit stories about her people and their traditions, especially about Earthmaker and the mischief-making Coyote. When Kit lost a baby tooth, Daisy assured her that she would have strong teeth if she dropped that tooth into a gopher hole. In the house on a cold day, Daisy usually headed to the warmest spot on the carpet to sit in the sunlight streaming through a window. It was the place for storytelling and to teach Kit games, especially the card game *Pedro*.

On their walks, always ready with a pocketknife in her apron pocket, Daisy picked young willow shoots for her baskets and bundled them into her apron to carry back to our house. She sat in her favorite place on the end of Kit's slide and distributed her harvest to Lilly and Kit as they sat on the lawn. One by one, they stripped leaves from each willow shoot while Daisy peeled off the bark. In the spring, the bark slipped off easily, but in the fall, Daisy carefully scraped it off with her pocketknife, exposing the inner white cane. Canes of similar size were sorted into small bundles, wrapped with narrow strips of cloth to keep them straight, and stored for future baskets.

Willow had multiple uses in the making of Daisy's baskets. It took many dozens of willow shoots to make a basket. Unique baskets woven entirely of willows were Daisy's sieves, strainers, and beaters called *lok som*. Other willow baskets with this open style of weaving were her small and large conical burden baskets, cradle boards, and other gathering baskets with handles made in a contemporary style. Willows provided the warp for twined baskets and the basic rod core for coiled baskets. When carefully whittled into thin strips, willows could be substituted for maple in the lighter part of the designs in coiled baskets.

2. Daisy Baker's *lok som*, a wicker sieve or strainer with a handle, made entirely from willows. *Photo, Pat Kurtz.*

At that time I was a substitute teacher and when I was home, our walks with Daisy and Lilly took us into the meadow and the forests above it to gather their traditional foods. Sugar pine nuts were larger and prized over most pine nuts. Other seeds, berries, cattail roots, and wild greens grew nearby. After a spring rain, I gathered edible mushrooms from our lawn and forest to include in my cooking. Daisy also gathered mushrooms. Hers looked different. I couldn't identify them in my mushroom book. She would not eat mine, nor would I eat hers. They gathered elderberries, chokecherries, and prickly gooseberries with their open weave willow *lok som*. Daisy placed one basket under a branch laden with berries and held the other one by the handle to beat the ripe berries off the branch. She spread the berries on a smooth rock slab and with a stone pestle smashed the fruit for drinks or pulp patties. After drying the patties, they were stored for winter use.

While smashing chokecherries, Daisy chanted quietly in Maidu:

> *He nesk ko pem, he nesk ko pem*
> *Boo hous chgna no, boo hous chgna no*

Translated: Eyeball, eyeball, knock it open, knock it open.

As a child, Kit foraged with Daisy and Lilly for *lop bom* (a wild carrot) and later wrote:

In the spring, just after the last white patches of snow have run away from even the deepest shadows, we look for *lop bom*. Lilly, Daisy, and I walk slowly across a pine-needle carpet along the old road near our house. Kaisi, my German short-haired pointer, runs from tree to tree. She is sure she will catch a gray squirrel. Carrying a basket to fill with lacy, dark-green leaves, we are sure we will find some *lop bom* for dinner. Lilly says that it might be too early as we search under the tall Ponderosa pines; *lop bom* does not grow in the meadow. Daisy is sure we will find some. I see some tiny eight-fingered hands of lupine leaves. Not *lop bom*. I run ahead and call Lilly and Daisy to look at the jewel like red of a snow plant. Daisy laughs at its beauty. The woods make her happy. Then Lilly reaches down and picks herby greens—*lop bom*. We found some. I run to more green under the giant cedar and more further on. Like Little Red Riding Hood picking flowers, we follow the trail of *lop bom* deeper in the forest. I am not worried though. These are our woods, and Lilly's and Daisy's ancestors searched here for succulent treats for centuries before we came. At last our basket is full, and bursting with pride, we follow the glow of the far-off kitchen light, eager to add our treasure to my mother's tasty dinner. I am sure that nothing she has will compare to *lop bom*. And, in the tradition of all good mothers, mine honors our gift by immediately cooking it up. I get plates and forks, and around the kitchen table we gobble delicious *lop bom*. It will be a few days before we will be able to find more. Too bad.

Years later, my mother told me that the *lop bom* flavor was so strong and herby that she could hardly swallow a bite. To me, in the first grade, it was a hundred times better than the canned spinach they served in our Quonset hut cafeteria. I will never forget the recess I missed while Mrs. Hall made me eat every last speck of canned spinach off my plate. Why she would also take that opportunity to drive home the importance of chewing each mouthful of food thirty times, I will never know. There is no accounting for taste. I'll take *lop bom* over canned spinach every time.

Our Friendship Grows

It was natural to include both Daisy and Lilly in our daily activities. We shared simple things and special events with them in our home. Though not obvious, similar values were woven through our experiences. We may have been "drinking from the same spring" as those parallels surfaced. Frugality was a necessity in the lives of my parents and an absolute necessity in early Maidu living. Cornell called himself "a child of the Depression." We used the native fruits, did not waste foods, and recycled household equipment.

We gave Daisy a worn wool comforter. Within a few weeks, she brought it back and gave it to Kit. Daisy had sewn pieces of used fabrics into a colorful patchwork and covered the comforter. Kit cherished this gift and slept under it for years. My mother and I made large braided and hooked rugs from used clothing we found at thrift stores. Daisy took great interest in Cornell's vegetable garden and wove him a strong, round willow basket to carry his harvests into the house.

Daisy's Christmas presents to us were her baskets. *Lok som* sieves, held our bread at meals. Her exquisite coiled baskets, incredible works of art, were a joy to behold. We received a small, coiled basket bowl with her bear paw design. For the following year, she gave us another bowl with a bear eye design. I admired a large, coiled tray with a tri-color, triple bird-wing design that she had woven in the past. She offered to sell it to me for twenty-five dollars. That was a lot of money for me, but knowing it was most unusual, I bought it. Respecting her beautiful work, we displayed it in prominent places throughout our home. Lilly made miniature cradle boards and gave Kit one for her dolls. Lilly's delicate lazy-daisy beaded necklaces were among her gifts to me. Our gifts to them were cooking creations from the kitchen, household items, and most often, new warm clothing.

3. Daisy Baker's large, coiled, tri-color basket tray, seventeen inches wide, 1940.
Photo, David Bozsik

Our holiday celebrations included them. When my parents visited, Mom, Lilly, and I would prepare dinner. Dad loved to play card games and invited Daisy to play *Pedro* with him. Having been taught *Pedro* by Daisy, Kit watched intently, because Poppie, her grandfather, had begun to teach her other card games. Daisy enjoyed these challenges. She recognized numbers, and with the opportunity to test her skills against the white man, she showed my dad that she certainly could count by winning a few games.

Though not obvious to me at that time, counting had to be basic for both Lilly and Daisy as basket makers. Basket construction demanded a high level of mathematical awareness as to the number of stitches and rows needed to build a three-dimensional shape with a particular surface design. Instructed from an early age, the weavers developed a sixth sense about these needs and innately knew when to add or decrease stitches.

Lilly knew when accounting errors were made on her small savings account, but would never question personnel at the bank about those errors. She welcomed my help to have them corrected. Lilly told us about placing gold coins in a bank for safe keeping before we knew her. She expected those gold coins to be returned to her, but when she withdrew the money, they gave her paper money. Feeling cheated and not understanding banking practices, she never trusted banks again, even though she continued using their services.

Early in our acceptance of each other, a simple incident occurred to tell me that discrimination toward Indians was the norm in our community. On one of our shopping trips to town, I thought that we might enjoy a nice afternoon treat at a restaurant on our way home. We entered and sat at a table waiting for service. Many people came in, were waited on, and received their orders. No one came to take our order. I soon realized what was happening, and I went to the counter and politely asked to be served. Only then were we served, but I was heartbroken over the incident.

Lilly's father's allotment, 160 acres of land, had been taken from him. It was said that his signature, an "X," had appeared on the sale papers. Up until his death, he claimed to have never signed those papers. In the following decades, the "authorities" failed to locate those suspect documents. This created a lifelong resentment and distrust between the Baker family and the Bureau of Indian Affairs.

The initial jury duty that brought us together lasted only a few days, but that seed of friendship sowed in the 1950s took root and grew throughout the following decades in unusual directions. Lilly moved in with us in 1970 and became part of our family for twenty-seven years, culminating in a fifty-five-year relationship. We responded to each other naturally, with an unquestioning care that bonded our friendship. Daisy and Lilly felt free to share vignettes of their past lives and expressed their desire to practice some of their cultural traditions.

Inwardly I found myself questioning the beliefs and actions of so many during this period in our nation's history, and wondered why the well-being of the natives was totally ignored. With some research, I discovered that recorded governmental acts revealed a national "mind-set"—to claim and occupy the western territories and to conquer the natives. We failed, as a nation, to understand that peoples of differing cultures could live side by side and appreciate each other.

3

A Brief Historical Background

Multiple land claims began as early as 1812, where policies by the US General Land Office (later the Department of the Interior) that covered swamp and overflow lands, encouraged western pioneers to claim and convert wet and unfit lands into viable agricultural ones. Additionally, in 1862, the Homestead Act gave pioneer applicants free title to 160 acres of land for agricultural development. The 1862 Railroad Act subsidized the building of transcontinental railroads, and from 1850 to 1871, railroads received ownership of more than 175,000,000 acres of land. In 1850, when California became a state, the federal government transferred the recording and management of "swamp and overflow" claims for reclamation purposes to the state. In 1861, California created a commission to monitor that process; but in 1866, the state abandoned the commission and handed the oversight responsibility to the county boards of supervisors. A large percentage of the Big Meadows lands were deemed "swamp and overflow" land. Unlike the 1862 Homestead Act, which limited acreage to 160, "swamp and overflow" lands under county control and supervision had no limitation of acreage for claimants. "Swamp land-grabbing" became rampant. Hundreds to thousands of acres in Big Meadows and neighboring valleys were claimed by landowners, as can be noted on the 1866 official Plumas County map, surveyed by V. Wackenrender under state geologist J. D. Whitney.

By the 1880s, the federal government felt concerned that Indian reservation life perpetuated indolence and the continued practice of Indian culture, thereby preventing their assimilation. In 1887, the Dawes Act, known as the Allotment Act, gave each Indian a piece of tribally owned land of 160 acres. The Indian, after owning and developing the land for twenty-five years, was bestowed a "patent in fee simple" with the rights and duties of citizenship. Allotments were granted to many of the Maidu living in Big Meadows and the neighboring valleys but not to Daisy Meadows. Daisy, her sister Rose, and their brother Joaquin were refused allotments because they didn't know who their father was. A considerable number of assigned allotments possibly overlapped swamp and overflow lands previously claimed by early pioneers. Along with poor recordation and sloppy oversight, this began an overture leading to multiple legal battles over questionable land ownership. The allotments were distributed nationwide, and it has been estimated that eventually 66 to 95 percent of Indian lands went to white ownership, leaving ninety thousand Indians homeless.

The Mountain Maidu, lacking a tight political structure with a designated chief, failed to negotiate with the federal government for reservation, ranchería, or allotment lands. Additionally, without adequate formal education needed to understand pioneer laws, they had little recourse to demand ranchería recognition. Gold rush pioneers had quickly claimed ownership of the lands rich with gold, silver, and copper ores that lay deep in rugged mountains covered with dense stands of marketable timber. Subsequently, even with the 1887 Dawes (Allotment) Act and its 1891 and 1906 Burke Act amendments that remained in effect until 1934, the Indians were considered squatters and trespassers.

The concept of a national forest service started in 1876, but it was not until 1891 when the Forest Reserve Act provided opportunity for the government to claim thirteen million acres of native forested lands. Acreage grew to include grasslands, and the government established the United States Forest Service in 1905. However, the vastness of western lands and with very little oversight of it encouraged mismanagement. Utility consortiums and lumber and railroad barons discovered easy ways to make fortunes under the 1862 Homestead Act by hiring unscrupulous individuals to stake multiple homesteading claims throughout the West. Not comprehending this unfamiliar concept of land ownership, the Indians lost their tribal lands.

4

The Baker Family of California's Mountain Maidu Country

Family Customs, Traditions, and Relationships

Maidu communities were family related, and several families often occupied the same dwelling. Before the pioneers introduced their social customs, Maidu customs were simple and basic. Birth dates, as white people recorded them, were not used by these people until the twentieth century. When a boy and girl began living together, they were considered married. Maidu leadership was not inherited. If they had a leader, they selected a popular or wealthy male, and he could be easily deposed.

They called their shamans—men or women—medicine men or prayer warriors. These people received high respect for their knowledge and their ability to use herbs and minerals in the healing arts. Possessing exceptional storytelling skills, they also interpreted dreams. Most importantly, these revered elders held the responsibility to carry forth their Maidu history through oral tradition and singing. Lilly expressed great reverence when speaking about her family's prayer warriors: blind grandfather Captain Baker Bill and Grandma Lucy (Baker). During these pioneering days, natives showing authority received some moniker representing a title. The natives often adopted their employers' surname.

Lilly Baker's Immediate Family

Lilly Baker's parents were Daisy Meadows of Big Meadows and Billy Baker of Taylorsville. They had five children. Jennie, born in 1892, was nineteen years older than Lilly. Ernest, the eldest son, was born around 1901. Rollin followed in 1906, Lilly in 1911, and Bill in 1914. Billy and Daisy followed a common Maidu practice and gave Jennie, their first born, to Rosie Meadows, Daisy's childless sister. Jennie and Rosie were five years apart in age. Ernest died when Lilly was a young girl. Jennie was not a basket maker, and she was the only Baker child to marry. She married Herb Young of Genesee. Herb was raised by his stepmother, Selena Jackson. All of Billy and Daisy's children were childless and had no immediate heirs to carry on their Mountain Maidu basket-making traditions.

The Meadows–Baker Legacy: Their Baskets

Besides their traditional oral history, the work of eight skilled basket makers, women from four generations of the Meadows–Baker family, expanded upon their family's records. Each weaver wove exceptionally well, using native materials for an individualized interpretation of the Maidu world as seen through her eyes. The women were knowledgeable botanists and mathematicians. Geometric images, stylized expressions of nature, were predominate designs in their coiled baskets and three of the eight weavers used vastly different butterfly symbols. Their work expressed astonishing weaving skills, with fine stitching, even rows, and uniform shapes. Designs of contrasting colors conveyed satisfying tactile and visual qualities. Each weaver, each basket, told a Maidu story. Each gift conveyed family history. Recognizing the remarkable craftsmanship of these women, collectors displayed their baskets in prestigious museums and institutions. Many of the fine gift baskets never left the family's ownership.

Weavers from the Meadows family of Big Meadows and Lake Almanor are:

Lilly Baker (1911–2006)
Daisy Meadows Baker (1879–1964), Lilly's mother

Rose Meadows Salem (1883–1969), Daisy's sister, Lilly's aunt
Kate Meadows McKinney (1863–1954), Daisy and Rosie's mother, Lilly's grandmother
Jennie Meadows (1850–?), Kate's mother, Daisy's grandmother, Lilly's great-grandmother, second wife to Big Meadows Bill

Weavers on the Baker branch of the family from Indian Valley are:
Lucy Baker (1859–1920), Lilly's grandmother, wife to Baker Bill
Polly Foreman Jackson (1882–?), cousin to Billy Baker
Selena Jackson (1874–1969), stepmother-in-law to Jennie Baker Young (Lilly's sister)

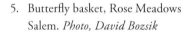

4. Butterfly basket, Daisy Meadows Baker. *Photo, David Bozsik*

5. Butterfly basket, Rose Meadows Salem. *Photo, David Bozsik*

6. Butterfly basket, Lilly Baker. *Photo, David Bozsik*

5

Big Meadows—Early Maidu Country

Daisy Meadows's Birthplace

Daisy sat in the front seat on our weekly grocery shopping trips from Lake Almanor to Greenville in Indian Valley. Three miles from home and above a steep cliff a mature growth of fir trees partially blocked our view of Lake Almanor. As we drove by, Daisy, while looking at me, often pointed down the cliff to the lake and said, "I born down there." I thought, *"Wow! Daisy's birthplace was in Big Meadows, now Lake Almanor, and she wanted her story to be told. Big Meadows Bill, a Mountain Maidu, was her mother's father—Daisy's grandfather."*

Early pioneers reported that Big Meadows was the most beautiful mountain valley that they had ever seen. At an elevation of 4500 feet and close to forty square miles, the rich and varied habitat was grassland surrounded by mountains 2000 to 3000 feet high. These ridges were covered with dense forests of pine, cedar, and fir. Exiting the meadow in the southern corner was the Feather River, which was formed by two branches, the North Fork from the west and Hamilton Branch from the north. Mount Lassen, a volcanic guardian towering over 10,000 feet, rose in the west. For centuries, this tribal territory was land that was "free and common" for all to use. From spring to fall, neighboring tribes—the Yahi, Atsugewi, and Achomawi—traveled to this valley for hunting, fishing, and gathering materials essential for their existence. Even though the Mountain Maidu had permanent settlements in this meadow, the severest of winters forced some less hardy families to migrate ten miles east to the lower 3500-foot elevation of Indian Valley.

Above the base of this south-facing cliff, Big Meadows Bill found an ideal location for his small family settlement. Low in the southern sky, the winter sun's rays gave radiant warmth to their dwellings and the steep slope above the settlement broke the flow of prevailing winds during raging storms. Fresh, clear water was plentiful. The two branches of the Feather River flowed through the heart-shaped valley, merged below the settlement in the southeast, and created a large falls named Salmon Falls. Scattered throughout the meadow, springs surrounded by willow clumps bubbled forth. Fish, deer, bear, small mammals, and birds were plentiful. Few black oaks grew at that elevation, but other plants provided an abundance of fruit, nuts, seeds, bulbs, and roots for food. Covering the western slopes, gigantic sugar pines, many six to eight feet in diameter, grew and bore large elongated pinecones. Harvested in the fall, these cones provided an abundance of tasty pine nuts. Gray willows and maples abounded for basket-making materials, and bear grass grew on the southern ridges.

Huge, thick slabs of bark, easily pried loose from Douglas fir snags, gave the Maidu building materials for their well-insulated, tepee-like houses. Smaller pieces of this bark supplied hot and long-burning fuel. The pioneers referred to this bark as "Almanor coal."

From Mount Lassen's slopes and in the northeastern lava fields of the Modoc tribe, all tribes collected igneous materials to craft tools. They chipped scrapers, knives, and arrow points from basalt and obsidian. The natives also found finer tool-making materials in the terminus of the Sierra Nevada along the eastern side of Big Meadows. These minerals—chert, jasper, and chalcedony— were highly prized for their multiple colors and luminosity.

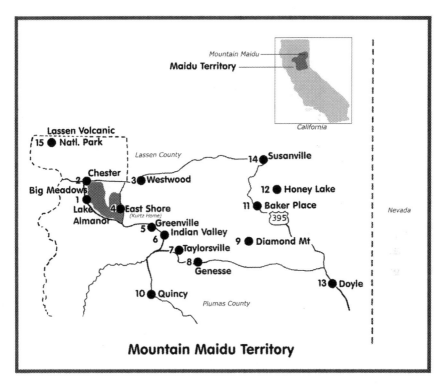

Mountain Maidu Territory

MOUNTAIN MAIDU COUNTRY in Northeastern Plumas County, California

The Meadows/Baker Family LIved in these places during Daisy's and Lilly's lifetimes.

1. Big Meadows - Lake Almanor - elevation 4500 feet.
Daisy Meadows' birthplace. Big Meadows Bill's family lived here.
Big Meadows became Lake Almanor in 1914
2. Chester - north end of Lake Almanor
3. Westwood - lumber town built by Red River Lumber Co.
4. East Shore - Salem ranch and location of Kurtz home
5. Greenville - Lilly's last home
6. Indian Valley - 1000 feet lower than Lake Almanor - home for many Maidu communities, including Patoot where Lilly Baker was born.
7. Taylorsville - Baker family's relatives lived here
8. Genesee - Bakers' first home - Herb Young's home
9. Diamond Mountain - Ridge separates Indian Valley from Honey Lake Valley
10. Quincy - Plumas County Seat in American Valley, other Maidu communities
11. Baker Place overlooking Honey Lake Valley
12. Honey Lake
13. Doyle - southern boundary of Honey Lake Maidu
14. Susanville - Lassen County Seat and Susanville Indian Rancheria
15. Mt. Lassen - in Lassen Volcanic National Park

Arrival of the Pioneers

The demise of the Mountain Maidu population, once numbering in the thousands, began when gold rush pioneers, led by Peter Lassen in 1849, passed through Big Meadows in droves. Before the gold rush, nonnative explorers had avoided this part of the rugged northeastern Sierra. Towering mountain ridges with canyons deeply cut by rushing rivers appeared impassable and forbidding. The tranquil subalpine valleys nestled in these mountains became isolated by winter storms. Peter Lassen claimed that his northeastern Sierra trail, perhaps an Indian trail, was a shortcut to the gold fields. It did not prove to be so.

Following Lassen's trail in October 1849, one of those pioneers, J. Goldsborough Bruff, recorded the following in his journals about the Big Meadows landscape.

> The water of the Feather River, one half mile below, as clear as crystal, bottom small pebbles and long coralline looking grass in it, adhering to flat rocks ... Numerous fish swimming about as leisurely as gold fish in a vase ... green grass, stately pines and firs, with their dark shade of green and yellow, the pale green willows marking the course of the stream and its branches. The tall mountains on the opposite side clothed with dark timber to their summits ... Great place for deer, cracking of rifles heard in the hills and woods, in every direction.

He further relates that men encountered grizzly bears. Big Meadows had a good crop of green grass for hay, and the pioneers took advantage of the opportunity to gather animal fodder for the trip ahead down Deer Creek Canyon. Bruff alludes to the fact that the Maidu were peaceful and friendly, and he wrote primarily of threatening encounters with the neighboring Yahi tribe after the wagon train left Big Meadows.

Most of the pioneers were headed to the wildly advertised gold strikes elsewhere. The few who stopped to settle in Big Meadows quietly pushed the Indians from their settlements onto marginal land. Lumbermen from the east claimed huge blocks of dense timber, built small sawmills, and supplied building materials for the towns growing around the mines. As the white settlements grew, Daisy's family was forced to leave Big Meadows. They moved east over Keddie Ridge to the lower elevation of Indian Valley and settled in the larger Maidu communities near Taylorsville. White farmers in both valleys raised beef and dairy cattle, provided food for the miners and lumbermen, and exported butter and cheese by wagon train to the Sacramento Valley and the mines in Idaho. In spite of the upheaval around Big Meadows, some Maidu families—the Henrys on the east and the Goulds in the west—remained to eke out their living.

As white settlements quickly grew in the last decades of the nineteenth century, Indian men, enticed by low-paying seasonal work, became laborers on the ranches and in the mines. As a result, they missed their traditional hunting and fishing times, and many Indian families became impoverished as the food gathering was left to the women, children, and old people. Naturally, with these changes, cultural practices were suppressed. Metal tools and implements replaced stone ones. Metal and wood containers replaced cooking and storage baskets. Fabric clothing and western footwear were readily accepted by both men and women. Interestingly, the deeply ingrained tradition of basket making held fast, and some women continued their weaving of utilitarian baskets for family use, along with the crafting of exquisite show pieces for gifting and trade.

6

The Bakers Move from Genesee
to Honey Lake

According to Daisy, before Lilly was born the Baker family moved about and lived in several locations in the Genesee Valley, just a few miles east of Indian Valley. Lilly's father, Billy Baker, worked as a farmhand on the Hosselkus ranch along with other Indians. Around 1900, the family moved to the upper part of the valley on a parcel of land that Billy had received as his allotment from the federal government.

Daisy sadly related, "Billy built a fine log house for me and three children. Soon he and two children got small pox. Two white people on the south side died. When we still sick, white men came at night and burned down our house. Don't know why." In that era, dwellings of persons inflicted with small pox were burned as a sanitation measure.

Left destitute and homeless, Billy Baker quickly built a smaller cabin on the site, but the family soon left and moved to a small Maidu settlement near Taylorsville called *Patoot*. It was nestled along Indian Creek against two unusually high earthen hills that rose abruptly from the valley floor; this became Lilly's birthplace in 1911.

Living in Indian Valley at Patoot hardly felt like a permanent home. Memories lingered of the torching of their Genesee home. Realizing that land and work were available in Honey Lake Valley on the eastern side of the Sierra Nevada, Billy and Daisy decided to move there. Lilly was a child, and Bill had not been born. With the help of relatives, the Bakers piled their few possessions onto a horse-drawn wagon. They traveled on an arduous wagon road heading east from Patoot. The seldom-used road, actually an old Indian trail, was rocky, rutted, and dusty. The difficult trip took several days: following a canyon over the Sierra summit, going past Antelope, and ending on the western side of Honey Lake Valley. The women and children walked, each one carrying bundles. Burden baskets, heavy on their shoulders, were filled with acorns and dried foods. Hot and tired, they welcomed rest periods at watering holes and the opportunity to unload their burdens to take a cool drink. The animals also needed rest. At nightfall, horses were unhitched and hobbled for an evening of grazing. Finding an open space, the men built a fire. Its dancing flames provided warmth against the cold mountain air and discouraged inquisitive forest animals from coming near the sleeping family.

After traversing a steep descent down the eastern slope of the Sierra, the family arrived in Honey Lake Valley. The trip had been long and tedious. They reached an entirely different environment than that of Indian Valley. The spring and summer seasons on the Nevada desert by Honey Lake were considerably warmer, yet spring arrived early and plants grew rapidly. Summers were beastly hot as a blue haze hung low over the vast eastern expanse of the desert. On the distant horizon, so often awash in cobalt and purple hues, temperatures rose and created mirages, making the mountain ridges dance slowly in undulating waves. Being rather shallow, Honey Lake dried up to a mere puddle, and the rushing creeks, the spring freshets from melting snows, disappeared.

But the Bakers felt a sense of relief as they surveyed the parcel of ground that had been given to them between the Will Bailey and Cornelius ranches along Jeter Road. Fifteen sloping acres, covered with grass and sagebrush under a scattering of big yellow pines, nestled below Thompson Peak and Diamond Mountain and overlooked the Nevada Desert. This was to be their home. The Honey Lake Maidu, distant friends, lived in small family communities scattered from Doyle to Susanville. Even though white ranchers treated them kindly, many days passed before the Bakers felt safe enough to build a new family settlement.

Getting Settled at Honey Lake

Billy Baker found work on the neighboring ranches. Other family members, blind Grandfather Baker Bill, the medicine man; Grandma Lucy Baker, the prayer warrior; and Bill and Kate McKinney, joined them. The men built permanent winter structures and outbuildings. Lilly spoke of their house as "the one built high because of frequent spring flooding from nearby creeks. It had access to the upper level with a ladder." This higher living space also prevented easy entry by unwelcome forest creatures. A nearby spring bubbled forth with abundant year-round fresh water. Firewood, collected from the forest above, came from branches and limbs blown down in the winter storms. Kerosene lanterns provided night light.

After the buildings were built, Lilly's elder brothers, Ernest and Rollin, left to work elsewhere and returned periodically to assist with family needs. In the following years, Lilly's brother, Ernest, and Bill McKinney died and were buried on the property.

Unable to read or write, both Billy and Daisy knew it was important for the two younger children to attend school. Billy signed important papers with his "X" and he, unknowingly, signed three different papers for the years 1909, 1910, and 1911 verifying Lilly's birth year. Lake District School was two miles from the Baker settlement, and Lilly rode to school bareback on their horse with Bill hanging on behind her. A white neighbor, Mrs. Cornelius, befriended Lilly and became her godsend. As a trusted friend, Mrs. Cornelius was well aware that Lilly desperately needed help with her schoolwork. Lilly stopped by after school and sat on the porch next to Mrs. Cornelius, sitting in her rocking chair, where she received the much-needed assistance with her lessons. No one in the Baker settlement possessed the reading and writing skills to help Lilly progress in school.

But the Maidu had the understanding of nature's signs in this unique high-Sierra environment, skills taught, instilled, and practiced by the Bakers' ancestors for generations. They knew instinctively how to manage their provisional storehouse with care. Rotating patterns in the night skies forecast seasonal changes, foretelling the times for hunting and for fishing and the times for gathering, digging, and picking. Earthmaker made it so for his people.

Basket Making, Harvests, and Hunting

Scoured by the rushing waters of winter and spring flooding, the basket-making gray-leaf willows grew profusely along the creeks. Gathering was seasonal, but the preparation process was ongoing. Family groups with neighbors took picking trips and gathered willow shoots by the wagon load. Lilly remembered these picking trips as happy times. Neighboring tribes, the Paiute and Washo, visited to trade their piñon pine nuts for these prized gray-willow shoots.

Each type of basket-making material required a different processing before it could be used. Sticky pine roots, so necessary for basket beginnings, became freshly exposed each season by rushing waters along the mountain creeks. Pieces cut off from main roots were split multiple times into useable widths. Big leaf maples grew at higher elevations in the pine forests. Maple provided the light background for the designs of coiled baskets. Gathered in the spring, maple shoots were slowly roasted over a low fire of coals and split repeatedly into fine weaving strands. Bracken fern roots were the fiber of choice for the black in the basket designs. On a nearby hill sat an old sawdust pile next to an abandoned sawmill where bracken ferns grew with unusually long roots. After harvesting these roots, women soaked them in five-gallon cans filled with a slurry of black mud to dye them even darker. Bear grass was picked on the mountainside above Greenville in the early summer; its season was very short.

Sitting on the ground together in the shade under a big pine, the weavers prepared their materials. Old and young, grandmothers and mothers, aunts and cousins, friends and neighbors instructed and shared ideas, sang and gossiped, teased and joked while watching, and even scolding, the younger children. Willow shoots were stripped of leaves and bark, sorted according to size, and tied in straight bundles for storage. Other materials, wound into layers of concentric circles, were maple strands, split pine roots, lengths of black fern roots, and split redbud covered with dark red bark.

Young girls learned basket-making skills during these sessions. As a child growing up in a family of boys, Lilly preferred to play and romp with the boys. She even challenged them in racing the family's horse.

Traditionally, only the girls had to learn basket making. Eventually, Lilly was coaxed to understand that it was her duty to join the women. Recalling her first attempt at weaving a basket, she said, "I didn't like the looks of it, so I threw it away. But my father found it under a tree, picked it up, and fixed it. He wrapped it in a cloth and pounded it with a rock into a better shape. He then insisted that I finish it." This first lesson in perseverance made a lasting impression on Lilly.

Harvest times—spring, summer, and fall—found all adults busy gathering foods. Women gathered seeds and nuts, dug for bulbs and tubers, and picked ripening fruits such as chokecherries, elderberries, gooseberries, manzanita berries, and native plums. When not eaten fresh, the fruit was smashed to flavor drinks or mashed and formed into patties to be dried and stored for winter meals. Oak trees, scattered throughout the upper pine forests, sometimes provided a limited crop of acorns.

However, black oaks grew profusely in Indian Valley. Acorns were "the staff of life" for the Maidu, and the Indian Valley acorns were considered the very best. In the autumn, the Baker family hitched their horses to the wagon, loaded it with supplies, and climbed aboard for a trip back over Diamond Mountain to Taylorsville. They visited relatives and caught up on the latest family news and gossip, but the main purpose of the journey was to gather a winter's supply of acorns.

The time-consuming preparation of acorns demanded care and patience. Meats from cracked nuts were removed from the shells, dried, and ground into fine flour on a smooth stone slab with a pestle or *mano*. Granite outcroppings on the Baker land became favorite grinding locations. Bitter tannin had to be leached from the flour to make it edible. Methods varied for this process. Daisy Baker spread the finely ground flour carefully on the flat boughs of incense cedar, loosely arranged over a *lok som*. She poured clean water slowly through the flour many times to remove the tannin. The flour gradually darkened and became a gelatinous mass that could be easily lifted off the boughs. Set aside to dry, it became flour again and ready for winter storage. Acorn soup was made in a coiled basket bowl by mixing water with the processed flour, turning it into a thin gruel and cooking with rocks heated in a fire. The hot rocks were picked up with two sticks and dropped directly into the gruel to cook the mixture. The basket bowl became watertight after repeated use as the basket's fibers expanded slightly and the acorn mixture sealed any tiny holes.

Men hunted for large and small game. Flightless waterfowl in their molting period were easily caught. Children hunted for and found eggs in the lake's tules and tall grasses. Fish were caught with traps and seines. Surplus meats were dried and stored in baskets for winter food and used for meals on long hunting and collecting journeys. Large animal hides, used for clothing, were scraped clean of hair and loose flesh, stretched to dry, and tanned by rubbing animal brains into them to make them soft and supple. Jackrabbits were numerous in Honey Lake Valley. When freshly killed, furry hides were cut into narrow and continuous long strips. As the flesh side dried, the strips curled inward to form long furry ribbons. While still pliable, these were woven into thick and soft blankets. Lilly fondly remembered her midwinter snuggling under a warm rabbit-skin robe after hot rocks, heated atop the wood stove, had warmed her bed.

(A photo was taken circa 1920 of the Baker family on their Honey Lake property. It included Daisy, Lilly, Billy Baker, young Bill, Rollin, and Ernest. Lilly was about eight years old. This photo has disappeared, but it can be seen in the DVD *Dancing with the Bear*.)

7
Recollections from Those Pioneering Years

It did not take long after pioneer contact for the Maidu to recognize that some cultural ways and traditions were impractical, especially with their clothing. Lilly recalled how the older women wore long Victorian skirts, the style of the times. She claimed, "I was a shy child. When strangers came and stared, I hid between my mother's legs and grabbed both sides of her long skirt and took them across my body like a cocoon. I felt safe."

While white people appeared inquisitive about the Maidu, most showed little respect and treated them as curiosity objects. Few efforts were made to learn the Maidu language. Communication was in English or sign language. White society's social rules created misunderstandings. Lilly and Daisy said that it was natural for Maidu women to pretend not to understand English, and they would speak only Maidu when questioned. Yet they had a great time giggling and laughing in Maidu over their private jokes. Mose Freeman, an often-quoted Maidu elder and Lilly's relative, gave wise instruction to youngsters by telling them, "White man talks, dummy up."

One incident underscored the cultural discipline of children. In Lilly's words, she related, "I was mean and used to have tantrums and cried and kicked the door when I had to stay with Grandma Baker. Lucy was her name. I had to stay with her before my brother Bill was born. She was a prayer warrior. I cried so much when she was busy rolling hemp on her leg to make string that she got disgusted with me. She grabbed me and put me on her lap. I slapped her. She reached down into her basket materials and got her awl, held me, and pierced my ears, then reached down and washed my face with water and prayed. After that I was good. I was the only girl in a family of boys.

"Grandfather (Baker) was blind and a medicine man. When he had a bad dream, he sat by a post and sang, shaking his rattle made of dried cocoons. He called his friends in, sang more, then interpreted the dream, talking about the spirit. I was always curious and wanted to see the spirit. I crawled up into his lap and listened to him sing, but I always fell asleep and never got to see the spirit."

During the late 1800s, wishing to teach English and discourage cultural practices, several pioneers in Indian Valley started small schools for the native children in their homes. Over the years, these efforts evolved into the Indian Mission School. The school grew considerably, and by the mid-1890s, the federal government took it over and ran it until it closed in 1922. From 60 to 148 students from the Maidu and the neighboring tribes boarded there each year during that time. The students were discouraged from speaking their native languages. Instruction focused primarily on training in the industrial and domestic arts.

At the height of the school's growth, the Baker family had lived in Patoot near Taylorsville. Daisy recalled, "The authorities were collecting and rounding up the children to put in the Indian Mission School. They took Jennie. Then Jennie got sick. Grandma Lucy (Baker) wanted to see her, but the school authorities wouldn't let her go in because she was a prayer warrior. But she did get in the school and cured Jennie. Both left, because Grandma Lucy cured her." By moving to Honey Lake, the Baker family avoided having their other children, including Lilly, placed in this school.

Some whites made sincere efforts to include the Indians in community life and a few whites even attended the Indian cultural events, but periodic misunderstandings flared into conflicts. Most pioneers chose not to understand the plight of the Maidu by insisting that the natives assimilate, learn English, and accept a European lifestyle. Many did learn to speak English, but few could write.

8. Indian Mission School in Indian Valley around 1918. *Lilly Baker Collection.*

Herb Young

Born in 1892 and growing up on the Hosselkus ranch in Genesee Valley, Herb Young was well aware of the anthropologists visiting and living on the ranch during the last decade of the nineteenth century. They were collecting stories about Maidu traditions, myths, and practices and Herb's father, Tom Young, fluent in English. gave most of the information to Roland B. Dixon, whose writings on the Maidu were published by the American Museum of Natural History in 1902. Nineteen of the twenty-one recorded Maidu myths came from Tom Young. Tom received two dollars a day for the information he provided to the anthropologists, while the ranch hands were paid only one dollar a day.

Herb's mother died when he was a lad. Her sister, Selena Jackson, became Herb's stepmother and raised him. Recognized for her exceptional basket weaving skills with fine, even stitches and bold designs, Selena's fame grew as one of the finest Maidu basket makers in the twentieth century. Herb respected her and cherished his collection of her baskets. A prestigious display of California Indian baskets in the 1915 Panama Pacific Exposition in San Francisco featured Selena Jackson's finest work.

9. Herb Young sits with his collection of Selena's baskets in Palermo, California, 1930. *Lilly Baker Collection.*

10. Selena Jackson stands with her baskets. Eight baskets in Herb Young's collection are in this photo. *Lilly Baker Collection.*

Well trained in Maidu tradition by his father, Herb became known for his singing ability. It was related that when Shim Taylor, a shaman from Genesee, wanted to retire and give up his shaman's rattle, Herb Young and Ernest Baker competed for the honor with their singing. Herb won. The Maidu believed that by singing a song repeatedly, the spirit comes to you.

Herb Young later married Jennie Baker, Lilly's sister, and they lived in Palermo near Oroville in the Konkow (Hill Maidu) territory.

8

The Bakers Move to Lake Almanor

Billy Baker Murdered

Lilly was thirteen years old when tragedy struck the Baker family. Her father was murdered in Susanville in December 1924. The death certificate stated that he was "bludgeoned to death by an unknown assailant or assailants." Molly, his sister, identified the body, and Billy Baker was buried on their land overlooking Honey Lake next to his son Ernest and Bill McKinney. According to the authorities, circumstances surrounding the event provided no clear evidence to discover the perpetrators. Years of legal entanglements followed and prolonged Daisy's inheritance to the property. It was sixteen years later, in 1940, before Donald Cady, a Susanville lawyer, and Judge Ben Curler, of Lassen County Superior Court, could present Daisy with a clear title to the Honey Lake land, which was valued at $150.

In 1924, the mourning Daisy Baker, with Lilly and Rollin, moved to a safe haven on the Salem ranch at Lake Almanor. Bill stayed at Honey Lake with relatives to finish school. The traditional mourning rituals of the cutting of hair and rubbing in pitch were not followed because white social customs demanded that it cease. Aunt Rosie Salem welcomed Daisy's assistance in caring for their ailing mother, Kate Meadows McKinney.

Rollin soon left to work on the ranches in Indian Valley. He had attended school through the third grade and claimed that "schoolin" just wasn't for him. But Lilly was approaching her high school years. The nearest school was seven miles away in Westwood, a prosperous lumber town built by Fletcher Walker, owner of the Red River Lumber Company.

Lilly Lives in Westwood to Attend High School

To attend school, Lilly had to live in Westwood and became a household helper to "pay" for her room and board. With abrupt cultural changes, she encountered many first experiences with indoor plumbing, hot and cold indoor running water, central heating, electricity, and different foods. She learned to drink milk instead of acorn soup. Meats were cooked on a stove, not in an open fire. Electric light bulbs, not kerosene lamps, provided light at night. People bathed inside—and often—with soap and warm water, not with cold spring water. Clothes were washed indoors and then ironed. Foods were stored in a box next to a big hunk of ice, not in baskets. Saying that she suffered culture shock would be an understatement. Entering into this new era as a teenager, she had no choice but to endure and embrace these contrasts without complaining. Cruel lessons disciplined and trained her. Once she failed to unplug an electric iron, and a child was burned when the iron fell off the ironing board. No family member comforted her.

Westwood was a company town. The Red River Lumber Company built the schools for the employees' children. The children came from mostly white families. As the only Indian in her class, Lilly's friends were few. Practically all of her Indian friends attended and boarded at the Indian Mission School in Indian Valley. Needing to feel accepted by her schoolmates, Lilly shunned controversy and always chose to be agreeable.

Dr. Fred Davis Sr. and Family

Lilly's primary employers were Dr. Fred Davis Sr., the lumber company's physician, and his wife Dora. They gave her some of the first lessons and training in "civilized" living. Lilly, coming from a family of prayer warriors and shamans, held great respect for doctors. Training with the Davis family launched her career in domestic services, which she followed after graduating from high school.

First hired by Great Western Power Company, Dr. Davis came to work in Big Meadows around the turn of the twentieth century. He was in charge of a small hospital at Meadow View, later called Canyondam, for the community of workers building the dam to create Lake Almanor. After Big Meadows was flooded in 1914, building activity ended, and Dr. Davis became the physician for Red River Lumber Company as the Walker family built their company town of Westwood in Mountain Meadows, a few miles north of Lake Almanor.

Reflecting on the past, Dora Davis often sadly commented that Big Meadows had been the most beautiful of mountain valleys that she had ever seen.

Well aware of the rich cultural environment around Big Meadows and Mountain Meadows, Fred and Dora collected Indian artifacts: weapon points, tools, and baskets. Grinding slabs, metates, and manos found along the lakeshore became embedded for the rock facing of the entire fireplace in their lakefront home. During the late nineteenth and early twentieth centuries, collectors assembled impressive displays of these Maidu artifacts. Professionals, including the Davis families, the Cadys, and Roseberrys of Susanville, welcomed Indian baskets as payments for their services. Baskets from members of Lilly's family are well represented in these collections that have since been donated to museums.

With an interest in the preservation of the area's history, Dora Davis persuaded Lilly to pose for her and painted a portrait of a young Maidu girl.

Lilly's work as a housekeeper for the Davis families in Westwood and then later in Susanville was fairly steady. Dr. Fred Davis Jr. (who was called Bun) was also a physician and lived next door to his parents with his young family in the late 1930s. Bun's wife, Alice, had befriended Lilly in high school. Lilly became housekeeper and nanny for their five children: Dorothy, Henry (who also became a doctor), Marka, Bonnie, and Paul. Lilly cherished memories of these years spent with the Davis families. However, when crises arose at Almanor, Lilly returned for brief visits to help care for Kate McKinney.

Lilly's Grandmother, Kate Meadows McKinney

From the 1930s to the 1950s, while Lilly worked as a live-in housekeeper and part-time nursemaid, her hands were seldom idle. In her childhood, Grandmother Kate encouraged Lilly's creativity and taught her to weave beaded neckpieces, purses, and bottles. When living with white people, with readily available materials purchased at local stores, Lilly embroidered on pillowcases, dresser scarves, and dish towels and crocheted afghans and tablecloths. Characteristic of many creative people, projects in various stages of development lay scattered about her room. Lilly's creative ethic to explore new ideas had been instilled by Kate McKinney.

In the early1950s, Kate McKinney's health failed rapidly, and she needed assistance just to get from her bed to an easy chair. She died in 1954, shortly before our first meeting with Lilly and Daisy. Kate was buried in the Indian cemetery along the east shore of Lake Almanor near the Big Meadows site of her birth. Kate had been a prolific basket maker. Her multiple and diverse skills surpassed those of many Maidu weavers. Yet in spite of the beautiful baskets and beadwork she crafted in her lifetime, the Bureau of Indian Affairs felt her estate was worth only seventy-five cents.

Lilly said, "Grandmother Kate's baskets were highly prized by collectors. Once she traded one of her very best baskets for a fine horse."

11. Kate Meadows McKinney traded a basket for a fine horse. *Lilly Baker Collection.*

Kate's unique weaving skills appear in both her coiled and twined basketry. Her large twined conical burden baskets have sometimes been mistaken to be from the Pit River and Hat Creek tribes. The Maidu learned the twining process from their northern neighbors, and these neighbors learned to make coiled baskets from the Maidu.

12. Kate Meadows McKinney, Lilly's grandmother, sits with her baskets and beadwork, 1940. *Lilly Baker Collection.*

Beads were introduced to the Indian tribes by the early pioneers. The Indian women quickly accepted these colorful materials in numerous ways by making sashes, neck pieces, purses, and covered bottles. Beaded ceremonial clothing often included pendants of abalone and shells. Kate McKinney was no exception and became a master at accepting new ideas. Lilly followed in Kate's footsteps with her beadwork. Her simple lazy-daisy chains, necklaces for women and bolo ties for men, were popular items sold at art shows.

Kate instructed Lilly in the making of beaded covers for small bottles, a time-consuming and complicated process. These decorative bottles had an important symbolic purpose. Used for burial rites, the Maidu filled them with water and placed them in the casket for the departed ones to use on their final journey. Beaded bottles replaced the traditional burial baskets filled with water. Along with this burial custom, the Maidu often cut the decease's possessions and placed them in the casket. When people brought Lilly broken baskets to mend and if she saw that the basket had been cut or burned, she refused to repair them. She said they came from a grave or had been retrieved from an annual burning honoring the dead.

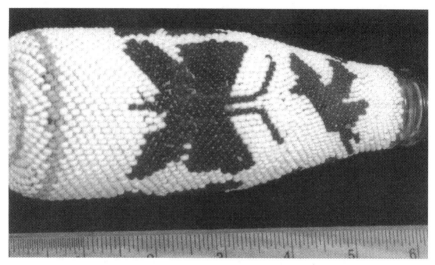

13. One of Lilly's beaded bottles with her butterfly design.
Photo for Maidu Museum, April Farnham..

During the transitional period from the nineteenth century into the early twentieth century, many of the Maidu people still preferred traditional products made by the women basket makers. Both of Lilly's grandmothers, Lucy Baker and Kate McKinney, made twine or cordage. They worked the strong fibers of a hemp-like plant by rolling and twisting them on their thighs. Twine had multiple uses. Large conical burden baskets that were carried upon backs and shoulders required protective rawhide strips on the basket's top edge. These were sewn on with the hemp twine. Carrying shoulder straps were also sewn to the firm rawhide edge with the strong hemp twine. Yards and yards of the hand-rolled twine were skillfully woven and knotted into fishing nets and seines.

Kate created small decorative chains from young hanging boughs of the Douglas fir. In the spring, needles and the bark on those limber stems peeled off easily. She coiled and twisted one fir stem at a time around a finger to form a strong link. Following the same twisting process, each subsequent link always included the previous one. Thusly, a fir-bough chain grew link by link. Kate made Lilly a two-part ceremonial outfit for her puberty rites by attaching numerous lengths of chains to a strip of fabric to be tied around the waist and worn like a hula skirt. A similar upper garment became a cape. Lilly kept this outfit for decades, but it disappeared during her last years.

14. Douglas fir chain links – ½" to ¾" in diameter. *Photo, Pat Kurtz.*

9

Modern Life Disrupts the Bakers' Maidu Traditions

Big Meadows to Lake Almanor

In the last decade of the nineteenth century, while the Bakers were still living in Genesee Valley, populations growing in southern California were demanding more electricity. Prospectors and entrepreneurs from eastern cities roamed the northern Sierra and focused their search on hydroelectric opportunities in the watercourses surrounding Big Meadows. Rumors abounded in the county newspapers concerning the activity of these strangers. By 1902, agents for Great Western Power Company had successfully bought a large amount of vital land, including the water rights that allowed them to proceed with plans to build an earthen dam at the river's exit in the southeastern end of Big Meadows. Subsequent flooding began in 1913, and with a heavy, wet winter in 1914, Lake Almanor became a recognizable lake.

Great Western Power's land acquisitions came with multiple guises. Reluctant landowners, unwilling to part with their holdings, forced Great Western Power to file condemnation suits against them claiming "eminent domain for public use." In 1909, without an experienced fire brigade and a missing alarm bell, the resort town of Prattville, located in Big Meadows, mysteriously caught fire and burned during their Fourth of July celebration. The townspeople and visitors were out in the meadow attending their annual baseball game. Some ranchers willingly sold to Great Western Power, as the well-established Stover brothers of Chester did and retained their land above the 4500-foot elevation. A few sales were negotiated out of court. Some homestead lands, swamp and overflow lands, and allotment lands were bought at fair market price. Great Western Power took six Maidu to court requesting condemnation of their allotments. One Maidu was Jennie Meadows, Lilly Baker's great-grandmother. In November 22, 1902, a trial was held, and the Maidu prevailed. The awarded judgment was the assessed value of the property plus an additional compensation of sixteen hundred dollars. Great Western Power paid them in cash, and the Indians "went home rejoicing." It was reported in a 1908 issue of the *Plumas National* that there was good reason for the joy, because the Maidu had never owned the land that had been condemned. Did these Indian parcels have multi-layered claims? Who can truthfully say that these Maidu never owned their native lands?

As the lake waters quickly filled the basin in 1913 and into 1914, many farm structures had not been removed. The Maidu, including Daisy Meadows Baker, watched their rich harvest lands disappear under the murky waters. All the grey willows, marshes with edible cattails and tules, fields of blue camass, and fishing holes vanished. Famous for rich runs of migrating salmon, Salmon Falls, near the dam site, became only a memory. It was not a beautiful lake. Water-soaked debris from dwellings, pastures, and outbuildings floated in the unhealthy, mucky water. Vegetation and tree removal had not been required by law. The man-created lake caused thousands of trees to die standing in the water, and massive piles of driftwood covered the shoreline. On June 14, 1914, Mount Lassen erupted with a fiery volcanic show and continued rumbling into 1920. The mountain god expressed disapproval for the destruction of Big Meadows.

By the mid-twentieth century, the uninviting forest of skeletal trees standing in shallow waters at the western end of the lake had transformed itself into a vast sanctuary for an incredible number of wildlife species, both birds and mammals. Even though game fishing for trout and bass had dramatically improved, big boney carp had become the predominant species. Large schools of these fish were harvested and brought ashore to a smelly building on the west shore called "the fish meal plant." Truckloads of fish were hauled to the Sacramento Valley and processed into animal food. On the west shore and in Chester, three Almanor fox farms raised silver foxes for the fashion industry and purchased this protein-rich animal food for their foxes.

Environmental Upheavals Begin Again

In less than fifty years, Lake Almanor quietly began to change again. Demands for electric power continued to grow. Lake residents, busy at work in their mountain communities, were unaware of construction activities proceeding at the dam. In 1960, Pacific Gas and Electric Company (PG&E), as the current owner of Lake Almanor's water, made preparations to raise the water level again. As reported in May 1970 in their monthly flyer, the *PG&E Progress*, "For years, Almanor's blue waters were marred in places by acres of snags—bleached skeletons of trees left standing in the reservoir a half century earlier. A decade ago, PG&E embarked on an ambitious program of removing these stumps. Four years and a million and a half dollars later, the face lifting was finished."

The phases of the project took several years. Concrete was pumped into the interior of Almanor's earthen dam to strengthen it. Federal and state regulations required the removal and disposal of the dead snags, shoreline collections of driftwood, and live trees along the lakeshore to the elevation of 4500 feet. Partial draining of the lake was necessary to aid the removal operations. Loggers on barges, loggers in boats, and loggers on the shore cut down thousands of trees. Floating trees were towed to shore, stacked with downed trees, and bulldozed into huge piles to be burned.

During this period of the clearing of trees and brush around the lake's periphery, all of the gray willows were destroyed. Daisy and Lilly quietly watched the destruction. Because of the future rising waters, the East Shore Indian Cemetery was to be relocated. Daisy and Lilly were notified that Kate McKinney's grave was to be moved to higher ground. Greatly distressed, they did not want Kate's grave to be disturbed. Believing that this desecration could be prevented, we presented their concerns before Judge Bertram Janes of the Plumas County Superior Court. He informed Daisy and Lilly that he had no authority to interfere with PG&E's plans. In a few days, along with the other Indian graves, Kate's remains were relocated to the new cemetery. Daisy and Lilly never visited the new grave site.

The landscape of Daisy's childhood kept changing. High-powered industrial equipment attacked the land, mutilated the vegetation, and stripped away its pastoral identity. Daisy sat watching with hands still busy in her basket making. Gray willows had to be found elsewhere. Fortunately, gray willows still grew along the Susan River, forty miles away in Susanville, and friends drove Lilly and Daisy over the mountain for their seasonal pickings. Why did Daisy continue her traditional practice? No one, no event, could stop her creative spirit and drive. Baskets were her soul food.

Archaeological Discoveries

Lowering of the lake's waters exposed vast expanses of land, revealing incredible opportunities for archaeological discoveries. In front of our property, we discovered evidence of a pioneer road that had passed through the meadow and the foundation of a blacksmith shop. Strewn around were pieces of forged metal, antique square nails, and a pair of beautifully forged sleigh runners.

Most importantly, thousands of Indian artifacts were brought to light. Jay von Werlhoff, the science teacher at Chester High School, took this rare opportunity to conduct and record a "scientific research" of the lakeshore by collecting all possible historical evidence before the lake waters were raised again. Teams of students searched the shore systematically and collected thousands of Indian artifacts. Some were perfect specimens, and many were broken. All gave evidence of active and productive early Indian life. Tools and implements, large and small, were of varied materials. Basalt tools told of older civilizations. Exquisite arrow points, sharp knives, and scrapers of many colors were formed from obsidian, jasper, chert, and chalcedony and revealed the exceptional skills and craftsmanship of the Maidu. When the "research" ended, the collections were sent to the University of California in Berkeley and have remained there.

After increasing the lake's level in the 1960s, PG&E funded a survey of the lakeshore in 1970, conducted by archaeologist Dr. Makoto Kowta of Chico State University. Assessing the historical value of located sites, Dr. Kowta wrote his report and sent us a letter recommending that we place the Indian spring on our property in the National Registry of Historical Sites. Filing guidelines appeared most stringent by limiting the use of the surrounding land. We declined to record it. Later an article in the *Chester Progressive* reported Dr. Kowta had discovered additional evidence in our meadow of Indian habitation.

10
Lilly Copes with Family Challenges

Sister Jennie Dies

During these environmental upheavals at Almanor, Lilly's brothers, Bill and Rollin, managed to find work as they needed funds. Being independent, they seldom stayed at the Almanor cabin with their mother and sister. In the warmer weather, they chose to live in the woods. Relatives and friends provided them shelter during the colder months, but Lilly always worried about their well-being.

Herb Young and his wife Jennie, Lilly's sister, lived in Palermo, near Oroville. Jennie became seriously ill in the late 1950s. Always ready to help, Lilly and Daisy moved "down below" to the Sacramento Valley to help Herb care for her during the many months of her lingering illness. Jennie died in 1958. Lilly and Daisy remained in Palermo to help monitor the wanderings of Herb's and Jennie's teenaged foster child, Lillian. The young girl often ran away and soon left home permanently. Lilly heard from her only when she needed money, and she eventually disappeared.

Upon returning to Almanor, the county welfare department "discovered" the women, living in their simple cabin built without insulation, using only wood for cooking and warmth, and drawing water from a nearby creek. An outhouse was off in the distance. This cabin was perhaps far more comfortable than many of their homes in the past, but the "authorities" told them that they were "living in poverty" and improvements had to be made for their welfare, including the installation of a propane stove for cooking and heat. Nothing happened. Lilly's brothers and the Salem men brought them wood as always. The spring water continued to flow past their back door. Not complaining, they kept busy with their basket making. They had no time to act or think poor.

Still Sharing Joy in Multiple Ways

Fortunately, during the 1950s and 1960s, resort owners and families living along the lakeshore welcomed Lilly's help. Daisy, with the drive of a true artist, continued to create and finish her baskets while Lilly's part-time resort work provided needed income. She was always ready to be a nanny or housekeeper for the Holscher, McMillan, Rich, Davis, and Kurtz families. Most interestingly, several of these families were families of teachers who had deep interest in the quickly-disappearing Maidu culture. Their children were most fortunate to have had the opportunity to experience snippets of Maidu tradition through Lilly's care and Daisy's presence. These children were Daisy's and Lilly's children. When people asked Lilly why she didn't have children, she shyly replied that she had lots of children and named these children.

Teachers in the local schools who knew of Daisy's and Lilly's basketry urged them to continue visiting classrooms to teach the children about the Maidu traditions. The teachers found transportation for them and included stipends. Both women thoroughly enjoyed giving the children hands-on demonstrations. Hundreds of fourth-grade students in Lassen and northern Plumas Counties had the privilege of shelling acorns and grinding their meats into flour with stone implements. They learned about basket-making fibers, prepared willows, bear grass, and maple for weaving, and sized fibers with sharp obsidian or a piece of broken glass. These were made pliable for weaving by soaking them in a basin of water, and the students even tried to weave on unfinished baskets.

15. Lilly Baker talks to students in a Janesville, California, classroom.
Photo, Herman Zittel.

In the late 1950s, my deep interest of the Maidu people and the history of the area continued, culminating with the recording of any and all information offered me. Inspired by Daisy's and Lilly's willingness to share their experiences and culture, I incorporated their stories into the major portion of my 1963 master's thesis for Chico State College: "A History of Indian Valley, Plumas County, California, 1850–1920." Little information had been published about this area of California. My research included interviews with other Indians and relatives of the early settlers, perusal of pioneer journals and scrapbooks, and the reading of all county newspapers from 1854 to 1920. My graduate committee publicly acknowledged the work was exceptional and timely, adding the recommendation that I continue writing about the Maidu, especially about Daisy and Lilly.

Close friends, Ardis and Philip Hyde, lived on Indian Creek near Genesee Valley. Ardis had been my college classmate, and we shared our family celebrations with Daisy and Lilly. Philip studied photography under Ansel Adams and had begun his career as a black-and-white environmental photographer. He recognized Daisy and Lilly's innocence and gentle charm whenever they quietly answered questions about their basket making. Knowing that they did not like to have their pictures taken, Philip still expressed a desire to photograph them working on their baskets in their home at the Salem ranch. They agreed to allow it if Philip included me in the picture-taking session. On one fall day in 1963, Philip photographed them. He worked quietly in the cabin's soft interior light, without creating poses. These records documented for posterity two Maidu women weaving traditional baskets—just as their ancestors did centuries ago.

16. Daisy and Lilly Baker working on their baskets in their Almanor home.
Photo by Philip Hyde, 1963.

17. Daisy Baker showing Pat Kurtz a cone-shaped basket. *Photo by Philip Hyde, 1963.*

Lilly continued to help me with my housework one day a week. Because Kit, Daisy's buddy, was attending elementary school in Greenville, Daisy always arrived with her basket-making work. On one warm and sunny autumn day, while the three of us were sitting on an old sheet spread on the lawn by the creek, busily stripping and cleaning willow rods, we had a surprise visitor.

An old friend, Charlie Yori, drove into the driveway in his ancient and battered red pickup truck. Daisy and Lilly tried to sneak away, not wanting to be seen. Charlie was a harmless and generous fellow, but he had the illusion that his Swiss–Italian charm was desired by all women. He would sidle close to give each female an unwelcomed kiss. Fortunately for me, I was tall and he was short. He had married Polly Gardiner, Lilly's home economics teacher, who had gained national recognition for her hand woven fabrics. Charlie looked old with scruffy graying hair and bronzed, weathered face. Amazing adventures had filled his life. He had been a "sourdough" during the Klondike gold rush, worked as a surveyor for the USGS in the Yukon, and knew the Lake Almanor basin better than most Indians did. He enjoyed telling us bizarre tales of unbelievable escapades.

Charlie had come to invite us to go huckleberry picking on the west side of the lake. I thought to myself, *Huckleberries? Are you kidding us, Charlie? They don't grow here.* But when Daisy's eyes lit up and a broad smile spread over her face, I realized she knew what Charlie was talking about. Standing up immediately, she shook the willow debris from her apron, folded the old sheet quickly over her willows, trotted into the house, and returned with an assortment of empty cardboard boxes. She was ready to go huckleberry picking—but not to ride with Charlie!

We three women climbed into my blue Chevy wagon, and as usual, Daisy sat in the front seat. I followed Charlie's truck along the east shore, feeling amazed that this surprise journey held no mystery for Daisy. She knew where we were going. Driving across the dam, we continued through the deeply forested west shore for about twenty miles. After passing the dirt road to the fish-meal plant, Charlie suddenly slowed and took a right turn onto a second gravel road. Not wishing to "eat" his dust, I lingered, driving through waist-high shrubbery beneath a grove of thirty-foot-tall lodge-pole pines. After parking the vehicles, we followed Charlie on foot.

An incredible harvest of huckleberries hung heavily on those shrubs, inviting us to begin our picking. Starting immediately, Daisy had her own system. She set her larger box under some branches, and with the smaller box, she beat the ripe berries off into the lower box, just as she would have used her wicker *lok som*. It was most efficient and fast. Our containers were filling quickly when Charlie called a warning. "Watch out for the bears!" Unaware that we were in bear territory, we looked around and saw bluish bear scat underfoot. Lilly and I agreed that there were plenty of berries for both the bears and us. With our boxes filled, we returned to the cars carrying a bountiful harvest of huckleberries. Charlie's bucket for Polly was overflowing. Daisy and Lilly giggled with delight over their gatherings. Upon returning home, after removing twigs and leaves from my collection, I put enough berries in the freezer for eight pies. All the while, I was secretly wishing I had seen a bear.

Sadly, this huckleberry patch along the west shore was cleared by PG&E in the early 1960s. The lodge-pole pines were cut, and the huckleberry shrubs were scraped from the land, bulldozed, and burned. The lake was raised, and Almanor West, a prestigious resort development, named this location Goose Bay.

11

Now Alone, Lilly Persists with Sharing

Daisy Baker Dies

After a brief illness in January 1964, Daisy died of heart failure in Susanville. She was about eighty-four years old, and we sadly missed her. Kit said that Daisy had been like a grandmother to her.

The three women close to Lilly—her grandmother Kate McKinney, her mother Daisy, and her sister Jennie Young—were gone. Brothers Rollin and Bill were seldom home, but when they were, brawls erupted during their drinking parties and these times scared her. Living alone and needing to work all day away from home, her possessions were not safe. Some items mysteriously disappeared. Her baskets were her only family records, each representing an important event with an individual basket maker from her extended family. Friends, including us, invited Lilly to store some of these items in their attics. Lilly even stayed with us for brief periods of time.

Shortly after Daisy's death, an unfortunate event occurred. While we were away for a weekend visiting my parents in Lake County, our two-car garage and shop caught on fire and burned. Fortunately, as the flames engulfed the building, a California State Highway patrolman happened to be driving by with his wife and noticed the fire. He immediately notified the fire department and began to fight the fire while his wife warned and directed passing highway traffic. Upon their arrival, the firemen pulled our Jeep from the burning building and kept the fire away from two fifty-gallon tanks filled with gasoline. The building and most of the contents were destroyed. Some charred items, blackened with soot, were salvageable. We had allowed friends to store their possessions in the attic. Lilly had stored her Grandma Lucy Baker's irreplaceable handmade hemp fishing nets and seines there, and now these precious items were in ashes. We were heartbroken.

In spite of the loss, and always ready to help, Lilly assisted with the cleanup. Together, we sifted through the debris with hopes of rescuing some precious item. With sweaty faces and greasy, blackened hands, arms, and clothing, we both agreed that this "cleanup" was absolutely the worst job either of us ever had to do. The cause of the fire was most mysterious to the fire chief. Three similar fires occurred in the neighborhood that year, none before that and none since.

The Kurtz Family Moves to Japan

Meanwhile, the water in the lake remained low for several years. PG&E's contractors continued the removal of trees and driftwood, and they worked close to our home. Gray willows and the forty-year-old yellow pines bordering our lakeshore were torn out. We did not own that land, but our deed gave us the right to use it. A picnic site that we had developed under the pines was demolished.

The vast expanse of the lakeshore looked like a war zone. Cut and fallen trees included unmarketable timber. All—the willows, timber, and shoreline driftwood—were bulldozed into towering piles, easily fifteen feet high, to be burned on our lakefront. Burning began and continued unceasingly throughout the fall of 1963 and well into 1964. Dense smoke filled the lake basin and settled there for months. The devastation, destruction, scraping, dust, and noise of the bulldozers created a traumatic atmosphere. Freshly cut trees full of moisture resisted burning and with a limited time schedule, contractors chose to bulldoze huge craters on the beach to bury the charred remains. We felt punished. Our beautiful lakefront view, now barren and scorched, was a smoke-filled landscape.

It was time to go elsewhere. In that summer of 1964, Cornell took a leave of absence from the Greenville Elementary School. Renting our home, we accepted offers to teach at an international bilingual school in Tokyo, Japan, and lived there for the next three years. During that period my dad passed on and my mom visited us for several months.

With Daisy gone, Lilly lived alone at the remote Salem ranch and depended upon others for transportation. She had no close relatives, and distant ones did not invite her to come and live with them. Invited to be a housekeeper again for Alice and Bun Davis in Susanville was her best option since Bonnie and Paul were still at home. Having worked for the Davis families off and on since her high school years, this move was the most logical one for Lilly to take.

12

We Return Home to Lake Almanor

Upon returning from Japan to our Almanor home in the summer of 1967, Cornell resumed his teaching in Greenville. I was offered and I accepted a position teaching remedial reading at the elementary school. I also taught evening watercolor classes for Feather River College in Greenville and Lassen Community College in Susanville. Kit continued her education in Saint Louis, Missouri. We all adjusted to our new routine.

A long-awaited desire of many years was to return my painting. It finally became a reality, and my work began to sell. Needing a gallery for sales and a room for summer workshops, we moved our two cars from the shop/garage and transformed the space into a simple and attractive classroom and gallery. Summer residents looked forward to creative opportunities, and the workshops were well-attended. Subject matter for paintings abounded: flower gardens, grassy meadows, wildflowers, lakeshore driftwood and a willow-lined creek. Kit, home for the summer, began to paint and soon taught classes in drawing. Besides framing our paintings, Cornell discovered his artistic expression and carved sculptures of local wildlife from soapstone found at an Indian site along the road to Buck's Lake above Quincy.

The Almanor Art Show

A highlight for the Lake Almanor summer season was the annual Lake Almanor Art Show on the first Sunday in August. Early in the 1960s, Norma Allen, owner of the Lassen View Resort, started the first show as a small and folksy gathering to encourage the vacationers residing at the resort to display and sell their artwork. It grew quickly. Works by local artists were added and it became a "must-see" venue for summer visitors. Craft artists displayed their wares on tables set under large pine trees and paintings were hung on two-by-fours nailed between the trees. For thirty years, neighbors pitched in to organize and manage the show; I was chairman for nineteen years.

We encouraged Lilly to participate as one of the local artists. She was still living and working in Susanville, forty miles away, and stayed with us during these shows. Her simple display was not flashy, but homespun, and included a few baskets, basket materials, and tools used by her mother and grandmother. Visitors showed interest in her work, and Lilly politely answered questions as she prepared materials or wove on a basket. Some people simply did not know what to say but with curiosity asked, "Are you really an Indian?" "Does your basket honestly hold water?" "You eat acorns?" Others expressed genuine interest and watched intently as she worked. Lilly underestimated the real value of her baskets. They were underpriced. Perceptive collectors, knowing that it was a rare once-in-a-lifetime privilege to buy a Lilly Baker basket, bought her work and placed orders for future baskets.

Some people asked Lilly to teach them to weave. However, no one took the opportunity, since the traditional experience required that first step of year-round gathering and preparation of the native materials. They were surprised to learn that each traditional material had a different role in Maidu basket construction, and they were unaware that willows provided the core construction: the warp. Bear grass, maple, red bud, fern, and pine roots were the woof, the weaving partners. Another artist in the show made dozens of attractive but far less complicated baskets using long yellow pine needles and raffia of different colors. Many viewers believed the commonly held myth that even the traditional Indian baskets were constructed with pine needles and raffia.

18. Lilly sat with her display at an early Lake Almanor Art Show. *Lilly Baker Collection*

13
Lilly Helps Us during a Time of Need

Cornell and I were traveling to Susanville in November 1969, and our car slid on a curve covered with black ice. The car rolled over several times, and I was not wearing a seat belt. The car was severely, but cosmetically, damaged. Cornell was not injured, and though alert, I was immobilized. Medics in the ambulance and the doctor who accompanied Cornell when I was airlifted to San Francisco for care, stated that I would not be able to help myself for the rest of my life. I was completely paralyzed. Among my many "get well" cards was a letter from Lilly saying that if I ever returned home, she would come and care for me. Her love and compassion made me cry.

After several months, I was allowed to return home to Almanor with a team of caregivers. Mom left her home and came to help with a neighbor. Being a physical therapist, he assisted Mom with my daily care while Cornell was away teaching. Lilly kept her word and came to help. She was living with Alice and Bun Davis in Susanville forty miles away, but Alice drove her to our home to allow Lilly to help us four days every week

Lilly and Mom developed an easy-going routine for my nursing care, and at the same time, they met our daily needs. Lilly taught Mom to count in Maidu. When I would slip low in the hospital bed and need to be returned to the top, together they would lift me up with the "draw sheet." Counting *sut tum* (one), *pan num* (two), *sop pom* (three), and on *chew yem* (four), the two women would lift me higher on the bed and then giggle. Besides having compassion, Lilly possessed innate nursing know-how and the necessary physical strength to provide me with skilled care.

A few weeks into her efficient four-day routine, Lilly arrived with an unusually sad demeanor. I sensed that something was terribly wrong. Eventually she told us that Alice and Bun's marriage had ended. Alice was moving to Campbell, near San Jose, and Lilly would be homeless again. With heartfelt concern, I responded immediately and said, "Lilly, our home is now your home. Come and live with us." Showing great relief, she accepted our offer.

Since Kit was away at school, Kit's room became Lilly's. Home only in the summer, Kit agreed to move into the studio apartment over the studio/garage. Cornell drove to Susanville to help Lilly gather her possessions packed in vintage cardboard suitcases of various sizes, pillowcases, old flour sacks, cardboard boxes, and a large ornate trunk. Lilly treasured this vintage brass-handled trunk; it was decorated with metal studs, had two wide leather straps over an arched lid, and locked with an etched brass clasp. When storing these collections in her room, she confided to us that she finally felt safe.

For the next few months, Lilly helped Mom with the housekeeping and continued with my daily nursing care. As a trusted friend, she came to live with us, but soon she became a bonded member of our family and lived with us for the following twenty-seven years.

Despite months of complete paralysis, I had prayerful expectancy and confidence that I would eventually be mobile and back to an active life. Within five months, I was able to move my left hand and arm. Everyone cheered. They insisted that I begin to paint again. Being dominantly right-handed, I struggled to paint with my left hand and made an important discovery. I learned what my beginning students had to learn. The hand holding the brush had to be trained. I struggled with the training of my left hand, and eventually I managed to produce some fairly decent paintings. By midsummer, I taught a watercolor workshop in the studio/garage from a wheelchair. Completely mobile nine months later, I applied for and received my driver's license and returned to teaching at Lassen College. Mom happily returned to her Lakeport home and walnut ranch.

14

Life with the Kurtz Family

Lilly's bedroom was upstairs next to ours, and we shared the only bathroom. As a team, we planned our household chores. We both did the housecleaning. I washed our clothes. She ironed them. I cooked our meals. She cleaned the kitchen. Lilly knew how to cook but not enjoying it, preferred not to. I sewed and made clothes for the whole family. Lilly's clothes were added to my sewing projects. Her favorite fabrics had butterfly motifs. Embroidered denim work shirts were at the height of country fashion in the 1970s, and I embroidered ours with wildflower motifs. Wildflowers—themes in my paintings—inspired the wild tiger lilies with monarch butterflies that I designed for one of Lilly's shirts. She wore it only on special occasions.

Lilly chose to care for the animals. Our animals had their chores, too. Keiko, our well-trained German short-haired pointer, protected our home from intruding forest creatures. She whined at night, asking to be let out for her midnight tour of the neighborhood to bark at the deer. Keeping rodents at bay, Koko, the cat, hunted and carried her victims to Lilly's feet. Keiko and Koko followed Lilly on lakeshore walks and guarded her as she searched the washouts along the creek for exposed pine roots and bracken fern roots that traveled through pine needle carpets. In the spring, Lilly picked Douglas fir tips to make chains like her grandmother's.

Neighbors living along the lakeshore looked forward to her visits and on the weekends, Cornell joined her on these outings.

19a. Pat and Lilly relax in the patio with Koko the cat and Keiko the dog.

19b. Lilly and Koko the cat admiring each other in the art studio, 1978. *Lilly Baker Collecton.*

Seeing Lilly with us, some people decided that she might be a visiting distant relative. That was all right with us. Asked about our relationship, and enjoying a joke, she giggled and said that I was her blue-eyed sister and Kit was a blonde Indian. There was no need to encourage Lilly to feel part of our family. We expected her to feel comfortably at home with us. On weekly Sunday trips to Susanville for church and grocery shopping, Lilly attended her Church of the Nazarene for services and their social events. She visited her cousin Goldie Shafer and caught up on the local news. We encouraged her to keep in touch with Alice Davis in Campbell, whom she visited periodically even though she did not enjoy the bustle of city life.

Mother Nature's ever-changing shows made Lake Almanor a beautiful place. Weather patterns fluctuated and controlled our outdoor activities. Wildlife, flocking birds, and visits from forest critters all foretold seasonal changes. Year-round animal residents left tracks in the snow, telling us of their presence. On one freezing winter day, we watched an awesome event from our living room. We knelt on the sofa in front of a large picture window facing the lake, and watched a bald eagle circling above a flotilla of hundreds of black coots. He dove repeatedly into the flock and clumsily tried to capture one for a meal. With each dive, the clever coots quickly submerged. Because of his repeated failures, we became his cheering section. Suddenly he hit the water and did not rise to fly away.

I screamed, "Cornell, get the canoe out, and go save him!"
Looking at me, Lilly's demeanor said, "Are you crazy?"
Cornell retorted, "And TRY to save that huge bald eagle? NO WAY!"

Bit by bit, the eagle appeared to sink deeper into the icy water. But he gradually and awkwardly lifted his drenching wings and rose ever so slowly into the air, clutching a bundled coot in his talons. His cheering section shouted, "HOORAY!"

We exclaimed over the beauty of lingering sunsets. Spring flowers, yellow potentilla, yellow iris, white yarrow, pink mallow, baby blue eyes, and spikes of white rein orchis dotted the meadow. Many of my paintings included these wildflowers. Back from a walk, Lilly would place a handful of yellow monkey flowers on the windowsill above the kitchen sink. We felt humbled and blessed with spring's beauty playing its symphony of renewal. Foraging deer made us erect tall fences to protect the vegetable garden. But as the newly sprouted seeds surfaced above the warming earth, songbirds flew in and found them tasty. Lilly told us that each creature had his special purpose. We had invaded their land. But she scolded the bright blue Stellar's jay as he tried to build a nest on a slanted ledge. Daily she shouted at him, "*Kaieskum!* Why doesn't he pick the sticks up and use them again?" when she grudgingly swept up fallen twigs from the driveway.

Cool summer evenings enticed us outdoors into the meadow to lie on blankets, gaze at the star-studded Milky Way, search for constellations, and count shooting stars. Screech and great-horned owls hooted. Poorwills swooped above to catch night-flying insects. Coyotes howled in the distance and Lilly said, "He's up to mischief." Soon the cooler breezes sent us back to the house.

As autumn arrived, aspen leaves turned to gold and maples turned red. Large flocks of cackling geese and tundra swans flew overhead in *V* formations. Some rested on the lake. Dozens stayed for the winter, even after the lake froze over. Lilly commented, "Long winter coming, squirrel put away many pinecones. Lake gonna freeze." Mount Lassen, covered by early snows, majestically stood above the distant Cascades. It was time to pick wild blackberries and elderberries for pies, and chokecherries and wild plums for jams and jellies. Lilly's *lok som* baskets were ideal gathering tools. We carried harvested vegetables from Cornell's garden to the kitchen in Daisy's large wicker willow basket. Some veggies were canned, some frozen, and others stored in the cool pump house for winter meals.

With the approach of winter, eight to ten cords of wood were required for the wood stove. Cut, split, and gathered from the national forest with a permit, wood was stacked on the front porch near the lakefront door. Snow often filled the entranceways to the house, studio/garage, and highway with several feet of snow. Light and fluffy snow from cold storms shoveled easily, but heavy wet snow from warmer storms broke branches and caused power failures and shoveling became a back-breaking chore. Finally, after years of waxing and repairing snow shovels, we bought a gasoline-powered snow-blower. Wow! That little beast demanded far less human energy from Cornell when paths needed clearing. When winter storms caused power outages that lasted for several days, Lilly was our natural leader in cleaning and filling the kerosene lamps and trimming the wicks. Containers of water were set aside for these emergencies.

Bitter cold froze the lake quickly at night with thick ice. During the day the sun's rays melted the surface ice. Night temperatures dropped and froze the lake again. Alternating night and day freezing and thawing caused expansion and contraction. The ice shifted, orchestrating uncanny wolf-like howling sounds. It was scary and Lilly retreated to her room.

Reviving Maidu Basket Making

Art activities continued regardless of the season when Lilly joined our family of artists. Lilly's heritage, her Maidu basket making, was most unique. We encouraged her to spend more time with the traditional arts. Rising public interest in Indian culture showed her that people honestly wished to know more about the Maidu. As that interest grew, Lilly slowly realized that she needed to represent her culture without her mother's help. She needed more confidence for her role as messenger.

When she moved in, Lilly had an abundant supply of redbud, maple, and fern root. The willow supplies always needed replenishing and occasionally we took trips to pick willows and maple and to gather bear grass. On warm days after a willow-picking trip, we sat in the cool shade under the alders by our small creek, striping and cleaning the freshly picked willow rods. The creek gurgled softly on its way to the lake. Screeching osprey circled high in the sky, searching for a fish dinner near the shore. We worked quietly. Our fingers pulled away the leaves and bark and then slid over the rod to feel if it was smooth enough for use. When cool afternoon winds stirred the aspen leaves and white caps surfaced on the lake, we retreated indoors to the studio/garage where, when stoked, the old wood stove cheered us with welcomed warmth.

20. Lilly showed friends how she works on her baskets when at home. *Lilly Baker Collection.*

Lilly's early projects were for the children under her care. They were miniature cradle boards holding little homemade dolls. Kit received one when she was a child. One style started with a hard to find slender V-shaped willow branch. The two ends of the "V" were tied together to form an arch. Placed across that V shape, and tied firmly along each side, evenly sized willow rods were laid to form a mat to support the "baby" on its back. The addition of a series of leather loops along each side allowed a rawhide strap to be threaded left to right, through these loops, to hold the baby on the platform. An additional mat made with fine willows fastened to the top arch became a projecting hood to provide shade and protection for the infant. The single projection at the bottom of the V allowed the mother the option to push it securely into the ground so the strapped-in baby could watch surrounding activity.

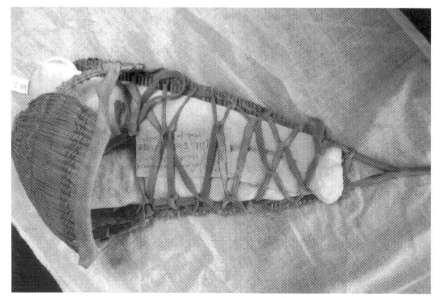

21. Miniature Maidu cradle board made by Lilly for Kit. *Photo, Pat Kurtz.*

Lilly's First Basket-Making Class

In the summer of 1973, Lilly taught her first class of non-Indians at one of our summer art workshops. It was a big step for her. She decided to teach the twining method of basketry. Her mother showed great skill with twining and wove a variety of twined containers including covered bottles, "what-not" baskets to hang on the wall, and fishing creels. Lilly struggled to learn this technique but eventually mastered it.

Arriving home from college and being familiar with Daisy's and Lilly's basket making, Kit enrolled in Lilly's class to give her moral support. Gray willows grew thirty miles away in Susanville and bear grass was nearby above Greenville. One week of daylong classes provided adequate time for the collecting and preparing of materials and the final weaving. From Lilly's cache of materials were pine roots for the initial basket beginnings and fern root strips for the black designs.

Years of instruction from her elders honed Lilly's basket-making skills. But teaching basket making in one week to students unfamiliar with Maidu culture was a new experience. She entered the role as instructor with great apprehension. Her desire to give each student a feeling of success with their first basket-making attempt was unrealistic. As her students encountered problems in handling the materials, Lilly lovingly took over the work and made corrections. She did not wish to see students struggle. She thought she should prevent it. Slowly she began to understand that students needed these problem-solving challenges; they were part of the learning process.

Lilly proudly said that Kit was her first student to finish a basket.

22. Kit's twined basket made from willow, bear grass, and fern root.
Photo for Maidu Museum, April Farnham.

In subsequent classes, few young Indians took active interest in mastering basket weaving under Lilly's tutelage. The gathering and preparing of materials were too time-consuming and tedious. Yet two students, Ennis Peck and Denise Davis, did devote time to perfect the craft. In the following decades, Ennis continued to develop his technique, and his innovative Maidu baskets gained him recognition for his fine work.

15
Echoes from the Past Revive Tradition

During the late 1960s and into the 1970s, the Indian friends and relatives who came to visit Lilly were primarily her brother-in-law Herb Young, her two brothers Rollin and Bill, and Ennis Peck. As a young man, Ennis would play the piano for Mom whenever she was there.

These four men were the only ones who would come into the house for the visit. In spite of our assurance that they were most welcome, Lilly's other friends and distant relatives politely chose to sit in the privacy of their cars and have Lilly visit them in the driveway. These visits were very important to Lilly. She and her visitors often conversed in Maidu.

Herb, now living by himself in Palermo near Oroville, maintained communication with the Bureau of Indian Affairs, hoping to gain federal recognition for the Maidu people as an active tribe. Part of his effort included the establishment of the Taylorsville Auxiliary of the INDIANS OF CALIFORNIA, INC. But the younger Maidu in Indian Valley were not interested in joining. Many memories from the Indian Valley Mission School continued to discourage the use of their language and the practice of cultural traditions. However, in the early 1960s, interest began to stir, and the annual spring rites of the Bear Dances were revived in the Plumas and Lassen counties.

The Taylorsville Auxiliary of the INDIANS OF CALIFORNIA, INC. owned a small meeting house with simple furnishings and a wood cookstove on the Greenville ranchería. But no other Maidu showed interest in joining the group. Herb and some elder members who lived in Oroville found travel to the mountains difficult. Lilly, the last treasurer, collected dues by mail and paid the property taxes. The elders passed on and no new members joined. Lilly, the sole remaining member, continued paying the taxes into the 1980s with her own money. With the lack of activity, the small building became vandalized and fell into great disrepair. Saddened, Lilly abandoned all effort to keep this dream alive and ceased paying its property taxes.

THIS IS TO CERTIFY THAT I,

Jennie Young, Rt. 2 box 2324,

Oroville, California. member of
INDIANS OF CALIFORNIA, INC., have paid three
dollars ($3.00) annual dues for 1957.

VERNON J. MILLER,
Treasurer

Enrollment No. 21917

23. Jennie Baker Young's membership card for INDIANS OF CALIFORNIA, INC. Taylorsville Auxiliary. *Lilly Baker Collection.*

24. Selena Jackson displaying her baskets with her niece and Jennie Young (Herb's wife and Lilly's sister), 1930. *Lilly Baker Collection.*

Herb Young still possessed great pride and enthusiasm for his Maidu heritage. He recorded his collection of Maidu traditional songs on reel-to-reel tapes. Herb was Lilly's most frequent Indian visitor, and he enjoyed lugging his bulky tape recorder into our living room to play his most recent recordings of Maidu songs. Though he sang of happiness, the coyote, other animals, and gambling, most songs were for the Bear Dances. In 1962, Gladys Mankins, a respected Maidu, held a Bear Dance at her ranch in Janesville near Susanville, and Herb Young sang his Bear Dance songs for the gathering. Everyone had a good time, but the elders complained that the young people did not dance "right." When Herb came to our house, Lilly embraced each moment and appeared enraptured by Herb's singing. Her eyes lit up. Evidently fond memories of family and friends stirred a sense of joy within her, and she said, "Prayer warrior Bob Tail always held the Bear Dances at his place in the late spring. It was a happy time with much good food, especially acorn soup and bread. Women danced separately from the men and sang while bumping shoulders and hips. They wore wreaths of flowers and danced. Wormwood was spread on the ground and in the creek for cleansing."

Somehow we felt like intruders, observers not participants, in their private cultural world. Having much curiosity and really knowing better, I asked Lilly to translate a song or two for us. She immediately appeared hesitant and asked Herb to do it. Her reluctance surprised us. We then realized that there might have been cultural reasons for this hesitance. Herb was the elder, a chosen shaman, and she respected his authority. We came to realize that although one could speak a language, providing a translation required a different skill, and Lilly did not have that skill.

Herb died in 1970, and Lilly inherited the big reel-to-reel tape recorder. She felt honored to be its keeper but then became distressed with her inability to use the machine. The equipment malfunctioned, and we assured her that it was not her fault. We lacked the skill to repair it. No one showed interest in the repair or in the historic tapes. All was donated to the Plumas County museum, and Lilly was told that the tapes and machine were given to the University of California.

Maidu Bear Dances

Even though Maidu Bear Dances had not been celebrated for many years, Herb sang and recorded his Bear Dance songs wishing that his recordings would be used for future revivals.

Bear Dances were annual spiritual celebrations. Fearing the bear as the main symbol of all evil and the rattlesnake second, the Maidu believed in the need to be cleansed from these two evils. Families traveled great distances to gather at the shaman's abode for this important spring event. They camped and brought food for feasting. A few respected elders and leaders fasted to increase their spiritual senses. On the morning scheduled for the "dance," these elders gathered at the campfire by the designated dance ground near a creek. They hung a long slender piece of maple bark from a pole, symbolizing the rattlesnake, as they sang and prayed to coax a growling "bear" to come from the forest. Covered with a bearskin, a man entered, growling with anger, only to be tamed with songs and prayers from the head elders. Cajoled, the calmed bear agreed not to harm the people during the coming year. Removing the bearskin and hanging it on a pole next to the rattlesnake signaled the dancing time. People danced while singing and shuffling their feet to the beat of rattles. Wormwood, known for its cleansing properties, hung around the dancers' necks. Women and girls decorated themselves with flowers and always danced separately from the men. The dancing accelerated and eventually ended as everyone went to the creek to throw the wormwood branches into the water as a final act of cleansing. After these days filled with joyful festivities, the people returned home feeling cleansed and ready to go out and safely gather food and materials for the year.

Even though Gladys Mankins began early Lassen County Bear Dance revivals in the 1960s, the location was changed to Willard Creek below Fredonyer Pass where the Maidu, Paiute, and Washo held their dances. The US Forest Service selected and named a campground for another highly revered Maidu, Roxie Peconam. Over the mountains to the west in Plumas County, Tom Epperson, also a respected Maidu elder, began his revivals of these spring gatherings in Quincy.

25. Respected elders prepared for a Bear Dance with Lilly's brother,
Bill Baker, on the right next to Herb Young on crutches.
CSU Chico, Meriam Library, Special Collections, Dorothy Hill Collection.

Lilly invited us to attend a Susanville Bear Dance at the Mankins place. Before leaving home, we gathered sprays of wormwood with Lilly. Wormwood, with its potent aroma, grew under the big old pine along our creek. Lilly tied the sprays into precious bundles to use for the "cleansing" near the end of the dance. Upon arriving at the dance site, we were relegated to a "kitchen" area to help prepare food for the attendees. We spent the day peeling buckets of onions and cooked potatoes, and made salads in large kettles.

People began arriving. Friends and families gathered in groups and happily greeted each other. Welcoming shouts filled the evening air as makeshift camps sprung up in the woods. Unfortunately, we had presumed that the traditional activities would commence in the late afternoon, but we were mistaken. People continued to arrive well after twilight. Lights from small campfires punctuated the darkness. Games and gambling started. But no ceremony began. Lilly disappeared, visiting friends from afar. Obviously, it was a time of joy and laughter echoed through the trees. It was late, and we were totally unprepared for sleeping on the ground under the starlit sky, so we sneaked away and left for the comfort of our own bed at home. We missed our first, and last, opportunity to experience a Maidu Bear Dance. Lilly returned home several days later totally refreshed and "cleansed."

These Bear Dance revivals gradually grew in number throughout the Maidu lands. Indians realized that their need for identity depended upon the survival of these traditions. Events near Fredonyer Pass soon included Indians from tribes elsewhere who introduced their traditions and attire into the celebrations; cultural practices became intertwined.

16

The Bond Strengthens between Lilly and the Kurtz Family

L iving with the Kurtz family during the early 1970s appeared to be a comfortable step for Lilly. She accepted our way of life, a life embraced by inherited European traditions. Even though Lilly's background had been firmly set early in her childhood by a native society of hunters and gatherers, she fell right into step with ours. Having lived the ways of her ancestors made Lilly a special member of our family. We never spoke of the differences in our upbringing

Loving her Maidu heritage deeply, Lilly well understood that her culture was quite different than ours. We sensed that she wanted acceptance from both the white and Maidu communities. Never married and in her sixties, she maintained her identity and carefully corrected the people who called her "Mrs." She firmly informed them that she was "Miss Baker." She wished that people would spell her name correctly with a double "l" and told some that "lily" was a flower and she was "Lilly." It never occurred to us that anyone would ask her why she never married or why she didn't have children. Being brought up with Victorian values, we respected her privacy and never inquired about her personal life. It was many years before we discovered that her father had been murdered.

The sharing of her cultural traditions with casual visitors seldom occurred, but when asked, she told her story naturally and briefly. On the other hand, even without her mother, Lilly's opportunities to share her Maidu culture and teach only multiplied. Her fame grew slowly throughout the state and rested gently upon her shoulders. Lilly didn't notice it.

Mom Moves in with Us

Early in the summer of 1973, as we departed for an art workshop in Europe, my mother announced that she had sold her ranch and was moving in with us in October. After teaching her first basket making class, Lilly went to Lakeport to help Mom prepare for the move. Their friendship had deepened, and it appeared that Lilly viewed Mom as an older sister. In spite of the need to pack, sort, and dispose of unwanted items, Mom held court in her kitchen by canning produce from her garden into jams, jellies, and pickles. As a second-place sweepstakes winner in the canned goods division at the Lake County Fair several times, she had to aim for first place. This was her last opportunity to prove her worth. Mom enlisted Lilly in the chopping, slicing, measuring, and, of course, the cleanup from the cooking marathon. Mom had decided to add ketchup to her list of entries, and a new challenge began. Her big kettle simmered with the thick, spicy tomato sauce. It plopped and bubbled like a volcano, spattering the stove, counters, walls, and ceiling with red dots. With two spoons, one in each hand, Mom tasted her brew and then that from Mr. Heinz's bottle. Soon her mix met with a smile of approval. Yes, it was a blue-ribbon winner, but it took days to scrub away those sticky red spots. This episode was a most appropriate farewell from Mom to her ranch.

Now three adult women lived in our home, and Cornell, being the only man, was most kind and caring to all. Lilly just fit in. We laughed and teased. Lilly and I talked about adopting each other, but we never could figure out how to do it and evidently felt it was not that important. Without question, gatherings and visits with our friends naturally always included Lilly. Seldom was a negative comment expressed from relatives as to why Lilly shared the dining table with us. We expected that everyone knew that Lilly was a beloved member of our family.

When deep winter snows kept us housebound, many evenings were spent enjoying the toasty warmth from the wood stove. Mom sewed on her quilt. Lilly crocheted afghans and taught me how to crochet. Cornell read to us, a most appreciative audience, from books he brought home from the school library. *Owls in the Family,* by Farley Mowat, provided many moments with chuckles and laughter. *Rabbit Hill,* for younger children, tickled the childlike harp strings in both Lilly and Mom, so much so that through the years, when preparing dinner for company, they'd call out a phrase from the book, "New folks are a'coming." In *Two in the Far North,* Margaret Murie wrote about growing up in Alaska and her adventurous first years of marriage living in the Arctic Circle with her new husband, Olaus. That autobiography made our cozy fire feel even cozier.

Mother coaxed Lilly to be her teammate for cooking sprees. Maintaining her reputation as a prize-winning cook, Mom hardly missed a step in trying out new recipes clipped from magazines and newspapers. My part-time teaching often kept me away all day, so Lilly became Mom's assistant. In spite of the mountains of dirty dishes, we held great expectations for tasty meals and treats.

Early spring months introduced the annual flurry of activity. Cornell plowed the ground to prepare it for his vegetable garden. Indoors, in the sunroom's warmth, seeds sowed in flats matured into seedlings. Dandelions popped up in the lawns, and Mom requested their tender greens be picked to be sautéed for dinner. Lilly said she preferred *lok bom.* Vinegar improved the dandelions' flavor, but when used fresh, they spiced up salads. Reading about cooking wild plants, *purslane,* a flat weed growing everywhere, caught Mom's attention. We said, "Enough!" It was slimy and hit the menu only once. Rhubarb stalks filled mouthwatering pies. Our big spring event occurred on Memorial Day weekend when we planted both seeds and seedlings in the garden and prayed for warm weather. Up went the six-foot wire deer fence around the vegetable garden with an old screen door for the entry. People asked Cornell, "Why the screen door?" The ardent recycler replied, "Why not? It keeps the bugs out."

Warm summer months with cool nights brought friends and family for short visits. After all, Almanor kept its century-old reputation of being a great vacation land. Cornell's vegetable produced an ample supply of salad greens, tomatoes, beans, corn and squash. Our guests relished meals from home grown produce and my art students enjoyed taking home the extra bounty.

During an autumn spawning season, the last journey in the life of the Kokanee trout, men from the California Fish and Game caught the fish and "milked" their eggs and sperm for the fish hatchery. These fresh trout were handed out, and news spread quickly of the fish "giveaway." Neighbors gathered and stood along the Big Springs shore to receive fish, each easily two feet long. Lilly and I stood in line to receive our two fish and returned home to clean and freeze them. Poking her head around the door, Mom said, "I want all of the heads, tails, and fins to make fish head soup." I thought she was joking, but Mom rarely joked. I thought, *How strange! I never heard of fish head soup when we were kids.* But Lilly understood Mom. The Indians used every part of the fish for food. Mom explained that when she was a child living in Dunnigan, her brothers caught salmon in the Sacramento River. Her mother always made fish head soup. Mom's face glowed at dinner that night. Aroma from her soup smelled most appetizing, and the soup was delicious. Smiling proudly with success, Mom said, "It tastes just like your Grandma's soup."

Lilly's First Trip East of Reno

Planning to continue her education at the Cranbrook Academy of Art near Detroit for a master of fine arts degree, Kit had to drive to Michigan in the fall of 1974. Lilly and I decided to accompany her and return home by plane. Lilly's mother had always wanted to go to Washington DC to meet "the great white father," and Lilly quietly admitted that seeing another part of our country would be an adventure.

Driving east from California, landscapes changed dramatically from our forested mountains to a bleak and treeless desert of the Great Basin. Lilly remained silent in the backseat. When asked, she did note that the expanses of the Nevada desert were "really big" yet similar to views from her Honey Lake childhood home. The pine forests of the Rocky Mountains hardly contrasted from those at home, but when the unending golden grain fields of the Great Plains appeared, they differed from the rice fields of California's Central Valley. Our family enjoyed singing while traveling great distances, and now Lilly understood the verses from "America the Beautiful" as we drove across the "fruited plains."

Warm and humid weather greeted us in Saint Louis. We visited close friends and toured the Principia campuses where Kit attended high school and college. As we drove across the rolling landscapes of Illinois and Indiana, the farms differed from the cattle ranches around Susanville. Forests of broad-leaved trees, still in green summer attire, accented the neat and orderly red brick buildings. In Michigan, Lilly met more family members and we toured the Cranbrook campuses.

After a couple of days, Lilly and I flew to Chicago from Detroit. It was Lilly's first ride in a large commercial plane. Her placid face did not reveal her feelings, but she said that she really wanted to see the really big lakes—the Great Lakes—from the air. It was cloudy. I insisted that she take the window seat, and I prayed for good viewing, but unfortunately the clouds allowed us only tiny glimpses of the lakes. However, when flying from Chicago to Reno, we were rewarded with spectacular views. The pilot circled and tipped the aircraft over the Grand Canyon, allowing each passenger opportunities to view the breathtaking canyon lands. Lilly appeared wide-eyed with wonder, but said little. I knew she treasured those moments as much as I did, as it was the only time either one of us would ever see the Grand Canyon. Arriving home after two weeks of traveling, Lilly appeared exhausted saying that all had been a dream. She seldom exclaimed when something unusual happened.

Questionable Retirement

During those years, Lilly had decided that housecleaning was her responsibility. When she was caring for me, we paid her the wages of a nurse. Being a family member, she had the option to select her own chores. Remembering that she had chosen 1911 for her birth year, and knowing that she arrived at the age to receive Social Security benefits, we encouraged her to claim them in 1976.

Presuming that Lilly would be delighted to be "retired," with no need to do housework, we realized that she did not understand it when we hired a new housekeeper, Leona. Lilly was insulted. Her feelings were hurt, and she sulked. Slowly adjusting to her new status, she then decided that it was her duty to advise and instruct the new girl. She was uneasy in the role of supervisor, but Leona understood and took the instruction with smiles. Lilly's good humor returned slowly in the following weeks as her new routine set in and she realized that more time was available for her basket making.

17

Making Baskets Alone at Home

During her lifetime, Lilly had known many of the elder Maidu basket makers. Now they were gone. Maidu girls lacked the desire to learn basket making since native customs disappeared. Gone was the necessity for woven containers. Gone was the need for gathering and storage of native foods. Without those vital requirements, traditional basket making developed into an art. Lilly began to realize the tragic reality of coming from a childless family as she sorely missed the presence of her elders, those experienced basket makers. Always working together, the elders had persisted in their basket making well into the twentieth century.

Privileged in her youth, Lilly received that training from the wise and revered elders. Those lessons incorporated years of keen observation with daily practice, mastering the art of survival with only the materials at hand. Through the centuries, women instinctively knew where to select only the best shoots from the gray willow, shoots coming from shrubs often scoured by the rushing waters of winter creeks. These shoots had great resiliency and perhaps a smaller pith. Kit remembered that Daisy always selected her willows from the same location on the shrub. The next year that spot would have many young shoots ready for picking. The elders may have told Lilly, "This piece of maple is better than that piece. See how it shines when split into a fine thread. It is so light and bright. Your maple shoot is too fat and

88

big. You need slender ones with no bumpy buds." Definitely, this warm exchange of ideas was the comforting relationship that Lilly missed. Lost to the past nothing replaced it. Without those elders to suggest or praise, without those experienced weavers to encourage or critique her progress, without the warm camaraderie of joking and laughing, basket weaving for Lilly was a solitary and lonesome occupation. Basket making had been more than "just" weaving. Each weaver, including Lilly, possessed an inner spirit of creativity, a drive of inspiration coming from within—a "sixth sense" directing the weaver in the process of creating each basket. This precious commodity goes far beyond verbal explanations for all true artists.

Two south-facing windows in Lilly's room let sunlight stream in onto her work area. Three big drawers below two large closets and an attic above provided ample storage for her materials and clothing. Basketry materials were strewn over the spare bed, ready for sorting and selecting. Long, narrow boxes held bear grass. Another held tied bundles of willow shoots. An old cardboard suitcase stored small coils of black fern root and red bud along with larger coils of split maple, all ready to be split again and again into the finest of strands. Split pieces of pine roots were bundled tightly with thin strips of rags. An old heavy aluminum pot with two black handles was her water container for soaking the larger materials, and a small stainless steel bowl held water for the finer strands. In a corner sat stacked boxes holding collections of tiny beads next to her assortment of miniature bottles waiting for beaded coverings.

Family activities allowed ample time for the artists to work daily. Lilly usually had a basket or two coming to life. She said that she had to wait for the basket to tell her what it wanted to be before work could continue. Ready to use, like the pigments on the artist's palette, her materials were muted earth tones: umber pine root, off-white bear grass, light-beige to ochre willow and maple, brick-red redbud and deep-black fern root. Just by handling the materials, visions of shapes and designs flowed forth mentally until Lilly felt one was "just right."

Basket beginnings were not easy. Forcing dampened willow rods into the tiniest of tight circles required a strong twisting force from her fingers, commanding the encircling sticky strands of pine root to hold the willow in place. A tiny reluctant coil grew, stitch by stitch, under her strong, gripping fingers. With each additional stitch, the basket's beginning slowly expanded as Lilly's weaving skills took control of the materials chosen for her project. Willow rods, carefully selected and sized equally, maintained the regular symmetry of each additional coiled row. Careful scrapping with a penknife sized the blunt end of each rod as it was individually added and layered to allow a smooth flow of stitches. When the stitching changed from pine root to maple, Lilly anticipated her planned shape and design of the basket.

It was hard work—a period of needed inspiration and a critical time for decisions. The weaver, Lilly, needed to focus as elements of shape, size, and design motifs that all came into play simultaneously. Shape involved deciding whether the basket should be a round bowl with straight or curved sides or a flat plate. Size dictated the future purpose of the basket. Motifs often told a story and could vary from wholly geometrical ones to shapes representing animals or other objects from nature. Traditionally, most designs were in darker materials, silhouetted against a background of split maple.

Stitch counting was essential. Designs in redbud or fern root against the light background were often repeated in threes. Her ability to mentally perceive what would be required in the following rows was constantly tested. Mistakes, if any, were unforgiving and if one happened, it had to be carefully removed. The most time-consuming, and requiring a critical eye, was the whittling of each stitching strand to a uniform width. Any variation of width detracted from the basket's symmetry and beauty. Ready for use, these strands, when placed in Lilly's shallow bowl, absorbed the water adding flexibility. Stitch by stitch, each strand was pushed through an opening made with a sharply pointed awl. One can only wonder how this skill was achieved in centuries past when the cutting and scraping tools were made of obsidian, chert, or jasper, and the awls were shaped and sharpened from dense animal bones.

Inquisitive people asked Lilly about the number of baskets she might have made in her lifetime. She was inclined to say that she had made hundreds of baskets. Considering the labor-intensive and time-consuming requirements for the gathering and preparing of materials before any weaving could begin and progress, her answer was incorrect. Realistically, she may have finished five or six baskets a year. But figuratively speaking, her answer of "hundreds" was absolutely correct. It was correct in the sense that just as artists paint pictures, they paint the same one mentally and with variations. Lilly visualized and mentally "saw" her baskets completed in multiple forms.

Viewers liked to know what inspired the designs. Was it an animal or a bird? Basket makers named some of their designs after animals or objects representing nature. Highly stylized and abstract designs defied identity. The basket maker might politely name familiar objects: snakes, entrails, animal tracks, feathers, flocks of geese, and arrow points. Some did not wish to name designs when geometric symbols, lines, and forms circled and flowed in oval patterns repetitively, pleasantly, and beautifully. The basket "talked" to the weaver and told her where the design should go. Lilly would say, "The design makes itself." Even the most utilitarian baskets would have some simple design. It wasn't unusual for the weaver to insert a "mistake," a stitch in another color or out of place, or add one colorful bead for a signature. Daisy did just that.

26. Lilly roasted spring maple shoots in an open fire at Lake Almanor in 1980.
Photo, Pat Kurtz

27. Lilly split spring maple shoots by an open fire at Lake Almanor in 1980.
Photo, Pat Kurtz.

18
Lilly's Family, Brothers Rollin and Bill

Family disappointments and tragedies tested Lilly's inner spirit throughout her lifetime. Never complaining, she naturally expressed and practiced a high sense of ethics, including honesty, integrity, kindness, and compassion. Family loyalty was important. After Daisy died, her only immediate family members were two unmarried brothers, Rollin and Bill. They spoke Maidu and shared a lifeline to the traditions that connected them to a past steeped in Maidu practices.

Their walking journeys took them to Greenville, Quincy, Westwood, Susanville, and Oroville. The brothers knew and understood the Maidu country. When not walking along the highways hoping for someone to pick them up, they took shortcuts, Indian trails over the mountains, and felt secure enough to sleep in the forests. Both men were personable and intelligent, but unfortunately, they were addicted to alcohol, and this increased while they served in the European theater during World War II.

Lilly always gave them the money they requested. She was proud of the fact that she never refused them funds. We, on the other hand, would offer them an opportunity to work in exchange for money. Bill always accepted our offer. He worked hard and long with Cornell building fences, splitting wood, or digging ditches. He was a good worker. Rollin preferred not to work, yet we enjoyed his company over a good meal and listened to many a tall tale. Both men, daredevils in their youth, claimed that in the winter they had driven eight miles across a deeply frozen Lake Almanor in an old touring car from the 1920s. Like many young men, they bragged of their foolish bravery hoping to shock their audience, and sometimes they did.

When infrequent robberies occurred at a summer home, it was not unusual for Bill and Rollin to be blamed for the deed. More than once, when the sheriff arrived at the Baker cabin on the Salem ranch to drive the men to jail, Bill and Rollin waved to their friends from the backseat of the black-and-white sedan. Summer residents happily shouted, "Hooray, the culprits are captured!" Bill and Rollin, not guilty of any crime, were also happy—they now had a clean bed in a warm dwelling with interesting bunk mates and three good meals every day. Neither one hurried to get out of jail.

Lilly's brothers, as with so many natives since the gold rush, experienced continuing upheaval and displacement from their lands. Compensation from the federal government tried to alleviate their losses with the allotments of 160 acres of land. These were often stolen, as happened to Billy Baker— Rollin's, Bill's, and Lilly's father. Billy Baker had been the recipient of an allotment that "happened" to become canceled on December 17, 1901. During his life, he denied ever signing a relinquishment to his land. Rollin later made repeated efforts to retrieve the land, and on January 13, 1926, he wrote to the BIA, further questioning this injustice and asking for their assistance. None came. Eventually, the BIA replied, stating that affidavits from certain authorities were necessary to prove the family's ownership. Lacking knowledgeable friends to guide his efforts to proceed further, Rollin did not continue to question these mysterious circumstances.

Rollin and Bill, and other Indian men, depended upon wages from irregular opportunities as itinerant laborers on ranches and in the lumbering community for their livelihood. Both men were inducted into the Army and served in the European theater during World War II and after their tours of duty were honorably discharged to join the unstable labor force once again.

Rollin Baker

When Lilly was caring for me as a nurse early in 1970, Rollin stopped by to visit me. He had such a gentle expression on his face. Unable to move at that time, I had been placed in a comfortable big chair, and Rollin sat next to me. With his hands covered, he said that he had a special gift for me and opened his hands to give me a small melon scoop with a worn, green-painted handle. A smooth, round pebble fit perfectly in the scoop. I was deeply touched by this simple and most unusual gift and tears rolled down my face. I imagined that Rollin had discovered the melon scoop in some old refuse pile, but he had searched hard and far to find that small, polished pebble to fit the tiny cup. This tender expression and recognition of simple beauty echoed that which we often saw in Daisy. (Yes, Rollin, I treasured that melon scoop, used it often, and placed the round pebble in our collection of Almanor gems.)

Neighbors along the east shore of the lake enjoyed visits with Rollin and Bill. One couple from Los Angeles suggested that Rollin might qualify for welfare payments, and Rollin promptly filled out an application for these payments. Monthly welfare checks arrived and were soon followed by a larger than usual back-payment check of several hundred dollars. It was a bonanza, and happy-go-lucky Rollin promptly celebrated with a party. He invited friends to join him at a nearby grocery store for a buying binge of liquor. After Rollin spent most of the money, the store owner telephoned Lilly to report the escapade. Questioning the source of funds, Lilly and I drove to the store, but Rollin and friends had disappeared into the forest. Nothing could be done. The store owner had the money, and the men had the booze. Shortly thereafter, Lilly received a call from the welfare department reporting that Rollin did not qualify for those welfare payments. He owed the department hundreds of dollars. They expected Lilly to pay for Rollin's misdeeds. I questioned them, "Did Lilly sign any of the necessary papers when Rollin made his application?" They replied, "No." I suggested that perhaps investigative research had been inadequate on Rollin's application and that Lilly was not responsible for their errors.

In December 1974, the sheriff notified Lilly that Rollin had died alone in a cabin behind a bar in a neighboring community. As a World War II veteran, his funeral expenses would be paid for by the Veterans Administration. Rollin's last Veteran's check was found on him and was spent by the undertaker for a fancy suit of clothes for the body and a classy casket. He called Lilly and asked her for an advance of two hundred dollars to open the grave and said that he would refund that sum to her within a few weeks when the VA funds arrived. Lilly and Cornell went to the funeral, and Cornell was a pallbearer.

Months went by, and Lilly waited for her refund from the undertaker. On one summer day when Lilly and I were having lunch in a local eatery, two men were dining at a nearby table. One was the undertaker. As he was paying his bill, I got up and walked over to him and politely introduced myself. I then directed his attention to Lilly, still sitting at our table. I reminded him of Rollin's funeral and of his promise to refund Lilly her two hundred dollars. He explained that the funeral costs went far beyond the provision of VA funds. I asked him if he had Lilly's signature for the additional costs. He answered "No" and proceeded to repeat his story. After the third explanation, I asked him if he knew the owner of a certain funeral home in Sacramento. He said he did. I told him that the owner was my first cousin (true) and that I understood about funerals costs from my cousin (not true). I repeated again, "When is Lilly going to receive her two hundred dollars?" Lilly received her money that afternoon.

Bill Baker

Lilly's brother Bill's health also declined. Being homeless by choice, he sought shelter with friends. Many were Maidu, and some were white men. Distant relatives usually welcomed him for brief visits. Soon after Rollin's death, someone reported to the Plumas County sheriff that Bill had been seriously ill in a boarding house for several days and needed help. The sheriff and Quincy's VA officer encouraged Bill to allow them to take him to Reno's Veterans Hospital for care. In spite of their excellent care, he soon died. Even though we drove Lilly to Reno to visit Bill in his final days, she was deeply distraught and felt responsible for the early demise of her brothers. They were the last members of her immediate family.

Her Family Collections

Lilly had not lived at the Salem ranch since Daisy died in 1964. Some of the finer baskets made by the Meadows–Baker women were stored at Aunt Rosie's big house in a locked glass-front case. Lilly, being the last remaining member of this basket-making family, realized that even if the collection was stored safely, she wanted these baskets in her possession. Aunt Rose died in 1969, and finally, in the late 1970s, Lilly had enough courage to ask for the baskets. They were returned to her.

Lilly had a personal ethic about gifts given to her. She never parted with any of them. Members of her immediate family had made and given her beautiful baskets. These treasured works of art documented her Meadows–Baker family history. Other precious items were her family photographs—pictures of her parents, grandparents, sister, brothers in World War II uniforms, and close friends. Gifts of trinkets and whatnots, clothes from all eras, a heavy mouton fur coat, elegant beaded dresses and bags from the 1920s, and Kate McKinney's porcupine hairbrush were all safely stored in that antique brass-studded trunk with other mementos. Once in a while, she opened the boxes and trunk to enjoy the memories these items evoked.

Long before we knew her, Lilly had worked for a family in Red Bluff and received two thousand dollars as a gift when she left their employment. She placed this money in a savings account, and it remained there for decades until her last years when she accepted care from the Public Guardian. Needing to spend it, she invested it in her prepaid burial plan.

19

Fame for Lilly and Her Baskets

Lilly's First Museum Show

During the '70s, when I displayed my paintings in art shows in towns and cities in the Sacramento Valley, I discovered Redding's new Museum and Art Center in a lovely park along the Sacramento River. Their attractive displays of California Indian baskets impressed me. Arrangements labeled with clarity showed deep respect for each weaver. It was obvious that the director, Marilyn Bond, and her staff expressed an unusual dedication for their collection and its preservation. .

Personnel at the museum had heard about Lilly's hands-on demonstrations sharing her culture's traditions. In 1980, Marilyn Bond invited Lilly to feature her family's baskets in a month-long show at the museum and to teach a three-day workshop in Maidu basket making following the opening of the show. Lilly consented. A two-part show included a Philip Hyde display of his provocative photographs depicting landscapes of the Maidu country.

The curators designed and built attractive display cases made of clear acrylic to hold the individual baskets. Each basket was placed on an acrylic stand and could be viewed easily from all angles. Oversized examples of twined and coiled techniques were crafted with acrylic rods and plastic ribbons offering the viewers additional visual information on the methods of the craft.

Displays of the Meadows–Baker baskets were arranged in one of the two very large rooms under the title, "LO LOM" TRADITIONAL ART OF A MAIDU FAMILY."

A second large and connecting room displayed Philip Hyde's impressive photographs, which were titled, "MAIDU COUNTRY—Many familiar and not-so-familiar scenes of Lake Almanor and Plumas County."

This was Lilly's first big museum show. To be featured with her friend Philip Hyde excited her. We bought her a lovely ivory-colored, silky dress to wear for the opening. She said it was the prettiest dress she had ever owned. We teased and called her "Queen Lilly." The happy occasion was a great success. Having her dear friends, Philip and Ardis Hyde, there made the opening reception seem more like a family gathering. The large crowd had traveled from all over California and elsewhere to honor both Lilly and Philip.

We returned home to Lake Almanor that evening and left Lilly in Redding with the museum staff. For the next few days, Lilly was tested by being in a strange environment. With determination, she busily taught her class, made new friends with the museum staff and workshop students, and felt some measure of success for her efforts. It was not easy. These students were white people, not Indians. For Lilly, this experience was a big step forward in a mission by opening the doors for a greater appreciation of her people.

Lilly returned home from Redding tired but happy to be back in her familiar surroundings. It was the first time she had taught classes without the comfort of family nearby to support her activity.

Dale Kronkright, the conservator of the Indian basket collection at the Redding Museum, recognized that Lilly's work and her dedication to share the Maidu traditions with her collection of family baskets were most unique. Dale became instrumental in arranging future displays for her with out-of-state museums. The first out-of-state show to include the Meadows–Baker family's baskets was the Nationwide Indian Basketry Show at the Kohler Art Center in Sheboygan, Wisconsin in 1982.

When Dale and other museum conservators handled Indian basketry, they did it with respect and great care. Transport containers were crafted individually from rigid blocks of Styrofoam. Cavities carved into a block fit each basket, which was wrapped in layers of soft fabric to prevent abrasion to the precious fibers. This extreme care was an eye-opener for us. Enjoying our baskets at home, we had displayed them on shelves, tables, and even on the mantel above the fireplace. When they became dirty or dusty, Lilly carefully washed each with warm water and Ivory soap and placed them in the sunshine to dry. Dale scolded her and explained that washing the baskets with soapy water was detrimental to the precious fibers. She welcomed the criticism from one with authority. His understanding about and appreciation for treasured Indian baskets amazed her.

Dale Kronkright wrote and presented an impressive scientific paper focusing on the Northern Maidu basketry materials. He presented it on May 29, 1982, to the Objects Group Session of the American Institute for the Conservation of Historic and Artistic Works. This insightful and in-depth paper discussed the practices of collection and preparation of the primary materials for Maidu baskets. The paper was a culmination of extensive research, but becoming acquainted with Lilly, her work, and her family's baskets through the Redding Museum show may have added verification to information he had already gathered.

Continuing Fame

In August 1982, Lilly was invited to be the honorary Parade Grand Marshall for the annual Plumas County Fair in Quincy. This was quite an honor. Her response was "Who? Me?" Plumas County citizens were beginning to recognize the value of their Indian heritage.

In 1983, Lilly and her basketry work, along with her teaching, became the focus of grants from the National Endowment of the Arts and the Plumas County Arts Commission. A small group of four students studied with her for a year. This allowed adequate time for their travel to gathering sites. As the early Maidu women did, they picked and collected seasonal native materials in the countryside around Quincy, told stories, laughed and joked, and prepared the materials before learning to weave baskets in the Maidu tradition. This yearlong activity was carefully documented with the fine photography of Sue Gutierrez. In the fall of 1985, the Plumas County Museum held a show depicting that year's study with Lilly and her four students. Displayed were the collected basketry materials, tools, and baskets made by Lilly, along with twenty enlarged black-and-white photographs and nearly one hundred color slides with descriptive narratives. A brochure titled "The Maidu Baskets of Lilly Baker" documented the study with photos by Sue Gutierrez and text by Jane Little.

As Plumas County and Lake Almanor increased in popularity as vacation locations, Lilly continued to give talks and demonstrations about her Maidu traditions to both visitors and local people. Shows around Plumas and Lassen Counties broadened her circle of admiring friends. Tour groups visited my studio and watched Lilly work on her baskets while I demonstrated watercolor painting. A large group of Japanese housewives came and were most enthralled with Lilly's work. The next year a tour group of Japanese therapists and health care technicians visited. Both groups enjoyed learning about Lilly's people and compared her to the indigenous *Ainu* of northern Japan.

When we were not directly involved, as with the Quincy Museum show and the study under the NEA and Plumas County Arts Commission grants, Lilly never ventured off by herself to investigate new and unfamiliar landscapes. When in the countryside to gather and collect basketry materials or traditional foods, she stayed within the boundaries of her Maidu territory. She enjoyed telling people, "I am not an Indian guide but an Indian basket maker." Never knowing how to drive or even having owned a car, she gratefully accepted rides and allowed others to make plans for her travel, meals, and lodging. She deserved this respect and care. Air travel, the purchase of tickets, handling of luggage, and the arrival and departure schedules were for others to decipher. She had never had to learn how to do these things, and it was easier for Lilly to accept assistance from those who knew how.

My mom passed on early in 1984, and we all missed her. With much to do in settling her affairs with my siblings, I kept busy. After completing the necessary paper work, I remembered that Daisy had often expressed a desire to see Washington DC. Now we had an opportunity to be tourists and visit Washington DC during the cherry blossom time. Our east coast friends welcomed Lilly as a celebrity. She was invited to talk about her Maidu people at a private school for gifted students in Chambersburg, Pennsylvania. A friend arranged for me to teach a watercolor workshop to a group of artists. We visited family and friends and toured the national landmarks.

A visit to the American Indian basket archives at the Smithsonian was planned for Lilly by Dale Kronkright. After viewing the public displays, a curator, Dale's friend, escorted us to a closed-off storage area of an immensely large building. We entered a room as big as a large gymnasium, filled with row after row of baskets from all American Indian tribes, and beheld immense collections in numbers far beyond any imagination. After walking through a maze of shelves loaded with baskets, we stopped by an area filled with assorted examples from the Mountain Maidu, whose basketry, according to anthropologist R. F. Heizer, "excelled that of any other tribe on the continent." Unknown to us at the time, Grandma Lucy Baker's basket was one of treasures in the Maidu collection. Their beauty impressed us, but inwardly we felt a sense of sadness. These baskets were hidden in an off-limits storage facility and could not be seen and appreciated by the viewing public.

20
Lilly's Health Fails

Shortly after the trip to Washington DC, when visiting with her friend Alice Davis in Campbell, Lilly became ill. She was sent to a Reno hospital for heart surgery. We were not privy to information surrounding the circumstances of this event. But when notified that Lilly was in intensive care in a Reno hospital, we felt shocked and surprised. We thought that she was visiting in Campbell. We had never known her to be ill or even heard her complain of illness. We promptly visited her in Reno and commuted daily to the hospital to monitor her recovery. Eventually we brought her home, and she was most grateful to be back in familiar surroundings. In the past, she had cared for me, and now we cared for her. Weekly examinations required that she be in Susanville to meet with doctors traveling from Reno. Each week, there was a different doctor and a different set of medications prescribed. Her slow recuperation caused us great concern. When she almost passed out on us, a local doctor scolded us for letting her take certain drugs prescribed for her by the Reno doctor.

A friend of many years, a pharmacist, told her that the Susanville ranchería had opened a new clinic. She qualified for their care and asked to be transferred to the clinic's doctor. Her health responded positively under his care. Having the same doctor each week, her medical needs were conveniently addressed and consistently monitored. Coming from a family of medicine men, she maintained great respect for all doctors and nurses. With great pride for her Indian heritage, she loved having Indian nurses assist her during clinic visits.

However, a hurdle was in place for qualification of their services. She had to prove that she was an Indian, even though she currently was receiving their services. At first, she thought it was a joke. They told her that, for some unexplained reason, her old BIA Indian enrollment number did not register and qualify her as a patient at the clinic. She had to obtain verification of her enrollment number from the Bureau of Indian Affairs on their stationery or apply for a new number. After decades of not trusting the BIA, she reluctantly complied and eventually received the verification in 1989.

Access to the free clinic thirty miles away in Susanville was a blessing for Lilly's continuing health problems. We drove her to Susanville for her weekly appointments. The clinic also provided transportation for patients who needed to travel to Reno for specialized medical services. Unfortunately, when these patients arrived at the medical facilities, they were "on their own." On one trip, Lilly was told that her glasses should be replaced. She returned home with an extremely expensive pair of fashionable glasses costing her $250. They did not fit on her full, round face. She explained that someone in a white coat told her to "come." Lilly followed, not knowing what else to do, and accepted the costly ill-fitting glasses without protest. We discovered that Lilly was alone in unfamiliar territory and had unquestioningly followed their suggestions. Replacements were eventually obtained, and we requested that the clinic provide assistance for Lilly on future trips to Reno.

Endowed with a great willingness to please everyone, Lilly's innocent and loving nature sometimes lacked wisdom when anyone made requests of her. She always agreed without realizing what demands would be required of her. She never said "No" to anyone.

21
She Remains under a Prolonging Spotlight

As the number of Lake Almanor's summer residents and visitors from Southern California increased each year, news of Lilly's basketry and demonstrations spread. Charles Hillinger, a well-known *Los Angeles Times* correspondent, called Lilly, requesting her permission to come to Lake Almanor to interview her for a feature article. She consented. He interviewed Lilly at our home, took her picture, and wrote an extensive article about her and her basketry, which was published on December 15, 1985.

In 1986, the University of New Mexico's Maxwell Museum of Anthropology in Albuquerque planned a show exploring the traditions of western Native American basket makers, titled "From the Weaver's View." Upon Dale Kronkright's suggestion, an invitation was sent to Lilly to participate. He felt that this show should have the Maidu baskets from the Meadows–Baker family representing California's Native Americans. Both Lilly and I were invited to Albuquerque with an all-expense-paid round-trip from Reno to attend the opening. Under Dale's supervision, a few of Lilly's prized baskets were again carefully packed and shipped to the museum. Arriving early, we watched the curators arrange the baskets under low light. With great interest, Lilly carefully observed the workmanship and materials used by other western tribes. After the evening ceremonies, we were invited to an impressive VIP dinner for the museum patrons. Not knowing anyone, we felt awkward in that sophisticated urban society, a bit like "country cousins." Even so, it was a good experience as it was another opportunity to be part of an anthropological display respecting Indian cultures.

Meanwhile, Linda Brennan, the director of the Plumas County Museum, wishing to share Lilly's knowledge of the Maidu basket-making traditions with a greater public, presented the idea of creating a documentary video about her. Grants from the museum, the National Endowment of the Arts, and the Plumas County Arts Commission funded the making of a video to be titled, *Making Baskets, Maidu Legacy: The Story of Lilly Baker*. Lilly signed a contract authorizing the video. It was decided that our home would be the center of activity. Plans formalized, and two young men were in charge. Daniel Voll interviewed Lilly, and Adam Horowitz, an award-winning filmmaker, was the cameraman. Linda Brennan planned the activities on a three-day schedule.

Lilly graciously followed their directions. She allowed the family's Meadows–Baker baskets to be arranged around her out in the meadow, with the lake and Mount Lassen as an impressive backdrop. As the question and answer dialog progressed, it became obvious that a simple knowledge of the Maidu culture was lacking. Questions became personal and asked little about the Maidu traditions or of the steps of their basket making. Showing the basket collection was most impressive. Filming continued at the Baker Honey Lake property, where Lilly's family had lived into the 1920s. One half-fallen building was visible on land overgrown with sagebrush, and the boulders with grinding holes were the only remaining evidence of the Baker community. Lilly was asked to show how her family cracked acorns and ground them into flour without the traditional grinding stones and winnowing tray. Lilly performed accordingly by cracking acorns with a small rock on a large boulder. In addition, as strangers often do when someone speaks another language, the young men took Lilly to visit an elderly friend, Elinor Wheelock, in the long-term care unit of the Indian Valley Hospital. They asked the ladies to talk in Maidu. Elinor was confused, but wanting to please, Lilly did her best.

The editing of the filmed material took months. Unknowingly, personal conversations with us, within our home, had been recorded and left in the film. We requested that these scenes be removed and they were not. Throughout our life together, when Lilly was involved with her Maidu activities and friends, we made sincere efforts to remain in the background and have her wear the Indian mantle and be the star of her show. Removing us from the video was important.

In 1994, the video was released with a surprisingly new title, *Dancing with the Bear*. With the revival of this Maidu tradition, the producers had added a few scenes from a Bear Dance in Quincy to make a more appealing introduction for the general public. Focus on Lilly as a Maidu basket maker was minimal.

28. Lilly worked on a basket in her bedroom at home. *Lilly Baker Collection..*

In 1995, for Lilly's willingness and dedication throughout the years demonstrating Maidu basket making and sharing her culture, the Soroptimist International of Almanor honored Lilly as the club's nominee for the 1996 Woman of Distinction Award, and her name was forwarded to the committee in the Sierra Nevada region. She emerged the winner, and in the same year, a confident Lilly Baker was honored at a special recognition luncheon in Las Vegas, Nevada.

22

We Yearn for Warm Hawaii

In 1985, we built and moved into a new solar home next door to our home built in 1952. The solar features of the new home made winter living even cozier and bright. With great relief, we had far less need to cut, store, and carry wood for the wood stove. Winter snows always demanded snow shoveling and plowing. The snows of '93 won an award as one of the big snows of the century. Cornell, retired from teaching, slowly found snow shoveling hard work. Lilly and I were of little help in that activity. I yearned for the warmth of Hawaii, my childhood home. I had not been there for over thirty years when my parents moved from Hilo to the mainland. Our creative ventures kept us busy in our Almanor art studio.

My high school class discovered me and invited me to a class reunion. We attended the reunion and took a sentimental tour of the Big Island, visiting my favorite childhood haunts. Looking at each other, we agreed with, "This is still a great place. We could live here." We became "snowbirds" during a few winter weeks over the next few years.

Lilly had traveled to Honolulu with Alice Davis to visit the Davis children. The landscapes of my home island, Hawaii, were entirely different from Oahu's. With enthusiasm, we invited Lilly to visit the island with us. I felt excited nourishing a deep desire that she must enjoy my tour. I hoped to "sell" her on the benefits of living there. Even though not charmed with the idea, Lilly consented to take the trip.

We arrived in Kona on the west side of the island, rented a car, and drove north to cross the island to spend our first night on the east side in Hilo. A breathtaking omen greeted us as we ascended the higher elevations of Waimea. As we entered a fine mist, a spectacular rainbow arched mightily over the road and enveloped us. Staying with us, it glowed brilliantly, embraced us, and led us up and over the pass. Those were speechless moments of overwhelming beauty and I secretly thought, *Lilly is going to love Hawaii.*

She showed no enthusiasm. Out of her comfort zone, she needed the cool, crisp, and dry mountain air to perk her up. We were greeted with *leis* at an event. Thinking Lilly was a local native, none were given to her. I was totally embarrassed. She informed them, "I am American Indian!"

29. Lilly, Pat, and Cornell vacationed in Kona, Hawaii. *Lilly Baker Collction.*

More than oblivious at the time, I later understood Lilly's discomfort. I looked back at my first years living in the Sierra. The arid climate dried my skin, and I was cold most of the time. I found the pine-clad mountains only green and bland, lacking the multiple colors and textures of Hawaii's landscapes. It took several years before I could deeply appreciate the unique beauty of both places. In Hawaii, Lilly saw multi-ethnic peoples, outgoing and amazingly loving, wearing skimpy and bright clothes, decorating themselves daily with flowers, and eating strange foods. All appeared bizarre to this child of the mountains, especially at the beaches. She did not know how to swim and could only watch the parade of sun worshipers: bikini clad swimmers wearing big black flippers and snorkeling goggles, and greased-up bodies lying on beach mats cooking themselves to a brown or bright red.

Still wishing to eventually move and become residents of Hawaii, we began to look for a home in Kona during our trips. Lilly decided that she would stay home at Almanor. We could not leave her alone. Someone needed to stay with her. Friends welcomed invitations to stay with her and enjoyed it. This arrangement was a satisfactory solution for a few years.

23

Moving to the Rancheria and Living Independently

Quietly and firmly, Lilly continued to insist that she would not live in Hawaii and, most importantly, she must live close to the Indian clinic and her people. Wishing to meet her desires and knowing that she could not live by herself, we searched for a care home for the elderly in Susanville. In the fall of 1995, much to our surprise, we discovered that the Susanville Indian Rancheria was in the process of building six small houses for their elders within walking distance to the clinic and eatery.

Each of the six small homes for the elders had two bedrooms, one bath, central heating, air conditioning, wall-to-wall carpeting, adequate storage areas, and even tinted windows. One hot meal a day was served to each elder at the eatery across the street. Lilly qualified for occupancy and eagerly filled out an application. To live in an Indian community appealed to her greatly. She had lived in Susanville for many years with the Davis families and was acquainted with many people. When completing the application, young Indian girls in the office excitedly said that they were going to take basket-making lessons from her. Lilly liked that.

The new house on the rancheria would not be ready for two months, and we were in the throes of upheaval with our move to Hawaii. A

Davis cousin, Bill Marshall, and his wife, Jane, invited Lilly to stay with them in Los Altos, and she accepted the invitation. Never wishing to be idle, she took her basket-making materials and made them a lovely basket.

In mid-December 1995, at the age of 84, Lilly happily moved into her very first own home. Mom's household items quickly furnished her kitchen, and we shopped for larger furniture: a dinette set, a sofa, a recliner, and a TV. She chose the living room's bright southern exposure for her work area. The second bedroom provided ample storage for basket materials, crochet yarns, and beading supplies. House plants cheered her space. After stocking her cupboards with needed supplies, she settled peacefully in her rocking chair and sighed, then smiled and added her soft, giggly laugh. Lilly was "at home." She had retained her sense of humor.

We organized a support team to help her. The county's social services sent someone to clean her house and do the laundry. Friends took her shopping, balanced her checkbook, and paid the utility bills, and we hoped that all her needs were met while we were away.

Lilly lived on the ranchería for the next five years. New friends were made, and a few of the younger people from Indian Valley drove to Susanville to visit her. Those who said that they wanted to learn the traditional Maidu basket making changed their minds quickly when basket making appeared to be tedious and time-consuming. They were unaware that working with Lilly was their "once-in-a-lifetime" opportunity to carry on a precious tradition. Lilly's gentle character did not include methods of verbal persuasion. No one in Susanville took her to pick willows, collect maple shoots, gather fern and pine roots, or gather bear grass.

The Light Still Focused on Her

In July 1997, the Oakland Museum held an Indian celebration called "A Community Festival, Maidu Big Time." Lilly and Ennis Peck demonstrated basket making in the traditional arts portion of the program along with the showing of the video *Dancing with the Bear*. Other Indian groups in the state began celebrating annual Bear Dances and called them Maidu Big Time. Ennis brought Lilly to these events to display and sell their baskets and introduced her to activities sponsored by CIBA, the California Indian Basketweavers Association.

The Lassen County Arts Commission Gallery in Susanville included Lilly's baskets in two shows. A show in November 1998, with a group of selected local artists, featured Lilly's favorite butterfly basket as the main attraction. Two years later, in 2000, they focused on this basket again as the main attraction in a California State Parks and United States Forest Service sponsored show, titled "Discovery Devastation Survival: Indians and the Gold Rush." Described in a news release, the show was "an educational Native American display that tells the story of the gold rush from the Indians' point of view." Funding was from various public and private sources.

When present at art and museum shows, "Big Times," powwows, and basketry demonstrations, people often took photos of Lilly. Some of them would graciously send her a copy. Once during a visit to the California State Fair, Lilly sat on a bench away from the crowds while we looked at displays. A photographer walked up to her and, without asking, took her picture. He then handed her five dollars. Her response was one of astonishment, shock, hurt, and "Oh, not again!" Someone took advantage of her solitary moment and paid her for the intrusion. We thought, *What could we do?* Lilly's face was a classic portrait of a Maidu woman.

The biggest surprise occurred in 1998. Mailed to every registered Democrat in the state of California was a colorful brochure promoting "Vote YES on Proposition 5—The Indian Self-Reliance Initiative." A full front-cover nameless portrait featured a wistful Indian elder. It was Lilly Baker! She did not know about this until a friend sent the flyer to her. She wished that the photographer and the Proposition 5 promoters had had the courtesy to ask for her permission to use her picture.

30. Lilly's portrait on the flyer encouraging a "Yes" vote for Proposition 5.
Photo from cover of Prop 5 flyer.

Lilly slowly realized that these incidents were the price she had to pay for fame. Without promoting herself throughout the years, students, teachers, anthropologists, university professors, writers, and ordinary people had plied her with questions about her basket making, her family, her Maidu traditions with its language. She had graciously welcomed each and every one as a friend, willingly provided requested information, and allowed herself to become a person of unusual interest for their numerous articles, essays, private and public collections, theses, and dissertations. Few persons returned to visit as her friend. Her story was told repeatedly, but her picking of willows had ceased. She could not see very well, and her gnarled fingers lacked the required strength for most basket making.

Lilly had spent a fair portion of her life patiently sharing her intimate knowledge of Maidu traditions. She still struggled inwardly believing that she needed to embrace two contrasting cultures. Her early Indian life, filled with the century-old traditions, had been simple and basic. She seldom spoke of those personal life experiences with their harsh and heartbreaking upheavals. The contemporary way of life was fast-moving, often confusing, and ever-changing with so many more comforts but all fraught with additional complications of laws and regulations. Her art made life vital and provided an escape from the public eye when needed.

24

Health Issues Require Outside Assistance

While living alone on the ranchería toward the end of the twentieth century, it was apparent that Lilly needed periodic physical assistance. Simple activities challenged her, from unlocking her front door to remembering if she had taken her medications. She fell, broke her hip, and was hospitalized for several months. Becoming frail, her memory became faulty. Always trusting everyone, she let strangers in to see her baskets. Soon some were missing, along with other important items. She couldn't remember who had been there. She asked a neighbor to help her locate missing items. They never found them. Her support team and housekeepers from social services kept changing. Our living in Hawaii during this time caused us great concern.

Lilly's situation was critical with her need to have a responsible overseer of her affairs available at all times. We enlisted the help of the Lassen County Public Guardian who became her most caring friend. In Lilly's ninetieth year, 2001, the ranchería management asked her to leave because "she might fall again and her family might sue us." Lilly did not have any immediate family. No distant relative ever came forth to offer her daily care. She absolutely did not want to come to Hawaii. We had to find her a home where she would receive that important day-to-day attention and love. It became most urgent to move her, the furnishings, and her personal effects immediately from the ranchería. We prayed for a practicable solution.

We discovered that a group of business people purchased the old, elegant, and slightly run-down Mount Lassen Hotel in the center of Susanville. They converted it into an assisted living establishment. Monthly costs were extremely pricey, but we were told that their state license required that a small number of low-income guests must be accepted for residency. Lilly qualified and became their first guest under that category. Moving her to a small hotel room required days of tough decision making. Sorting and packing became a soul-wrenching experience. No one from the ranchería or elsewhere offered to help. The small hotel room had space for one bed, a chest of drawers, her recliner, small side tables, and a TV; it had a bathroom that had to be shared with a neighbor in an adjoining room. The surplus possessions, including the antique trunk with the arched lid and boxes filled with basket-making materials, were stored in the hotel's basement. Lilly was not happy with the small space.

However, upon her move into the hotel, everyone on the staff immediately embraced Lilly's gentleness and grace. Their sincere efforts to have her feel at home included a nurse to administer her medications. Tasty meals were served in an elegant dining room. Each table was set with white linen cloths, silverware, colorful china, and a vase with fresh flowers. Besides keeping the residents busy, planned activities allowed them to become acquainted. Guests were required to sign in and state the purpose of the visit. Because of that rule, few Indian friends came to visit her.

Within the year, Lilly had a new neighbor, Viola Bowen. The two women could not believe their luck. Viola, Herb Young's cousin, and Lilly had been girlhood chums. The two neighbors bonded quickly. They were two Indians living in that big old hotel built by the white folk when in the past Indians were discouraged from entering. Viola and Lilly were buddies again and roommates for the next five years.

During these twilight years, the Public Guardian had complete charge over Lilly's affairs. He was compassionate and faithful in his care for both women. Within three years, the Mount Lassen Assisted Living was unable to meet the expected occupancy. The business failed and the establishment closed. The Alturas Long Term Care Facility in Modoc County had the only vacant beds for Lilly and Viola's relocation, and the Public Guardian moved them there. It was far from Susanville and even farther from Indian Valley for any of their friends to visit them. But fortune shone on the two ladies, and within a year, beds became available at the Indian Valley Hospital's Long Care Facility. Lilly was delighted for the move to Greenville near the place of her birth.

25
Farewell to Lilly

Even though Lilly's memory appeared to be failing, her sweet smile and gentle laugh enamored many a person. The nurses loved her. When Viola passed on, Lilly hardly noticed. She did not remember us when we visited. We still cherished the years of our friendship. We had shared so many special occasions together. Just the fact that we, as a family, valued her very being was all that mattered.

31. Lilly says good-bye to Lake Almanor and the geese gathering in the meadow to head south. *Photo, Irmgard Latham.*

Practicing our art together for so many years, we respected and understood each other's creativity and admired the sharing of the Maidu culture with others. Her simple innocence, her lack of sophistication, her joy, and her quiet laughter, along with Daisy's, are our treasured gifts. A Maidu relative quoted Lilly, who said that her mother told her, "Those people, the Kurtz family, have stolen my heart. Go stay with them." Daisy and Lilly also stole our hearts.

The sun set on Lilly's life. She passed away on November 3, 2006, at the Long Term Care Facility at the Indian Valley Hospital in Greenville, California. For the lack of funds, the hospital closed its doors the following month.

Lilly Baker was the last of the Mountain Maidu women to make traditional baskets.

Epilogue

A question arises, asking, "Does the traditional Maidu culture have a purpose in today's society?"

My answer is, "Yes." People from ethnic backgrounds yearn for a sense of identity. Most cultural traditions nurture an inner pride when reflecting upon a history telling of prosperity in centuries past. The fact remains that these Maidu used their keen understanding and knowledge of nature beneficially in a most hostile environment. With incredible skills, they flourished by utilizing every aspect of the available resources—the flora, fauna, and minerals—for their livelihood and existence. As peaceful and genial natives, they had numbered into the thousands when the gold rush pioneers entered and overran the rugged mountain environment to exploit its resources. Only then did their numbers decrease as changes in their traditional and cultural lifestyles occurred.

Within the past century, many people of Maidu ancestry earned and achieved commendable positions, serving society as nurses, doctors, servicemen, teachers, activists, artists, writers, and more. As a Mountain Maidu and an artist for over a half of a century, Lilly Baker became a messenger for her people. Coming from a traditional upbringing, she persisted, first with her mother Daisy and then alone, by giving those hands-on demonstrations of Maidu traditions to hundreds, perhaps thousands, of individuals in schools and civic groups. Clad in a mantle of quiet pride, she represented her people. Her unique act was not a "side show" but a celebration of the simple and primitive life that her family actually had lived, giving evidence that Maidu life was about far more than just survival.

Currently, a legacy for us exists in a collection of dozens of baskets, materials, tools, and other nineteenth and twentieth century artifacts representing the work of eight women basket makers from four generations of the Meadows–Baker family. Respect and admiration for these women is well deserved. Each item, so often seen only as an art object or antique, actually tells a larger and seldom-perceived life story.

Displayed at the Maidu Museum and Historical Site in Roseville, California, this collection has been rightly named "Our Precious Legacy." An illustrated catalog was published for the museum. In 1969, Roseville's city fathers purchased forty acres of Nisenan (Valley Maidu) lands— including petroglyphs, acorn-grinding cavities, and rolling grasslands with oak trees—from the federal government at one hundred dollars per acre. As a historical site, thirty acres were placed on the National Register of Historic Places. The new ten-thousand-square-foot museum, designed to represent an Indian round house, opened in February 2010.

What Daisy and Lilly Baker did quietly and graciously during their lifetimes by sharing their Maidu traditions and culture is worthy history. Admittedly, for this story, chronological gaps of Lilly's middle years exist. Inquiries were made of those who knew Lilly during the 1930s into the 1950s, and replies were minimal for the requested information. Presumably, these acquaintances did not wish to allow their experiences to be recorded.

Why did Daisy and Lilly continue with more than fifty years of sharing? This was their oral history—to teach and demonstrate what they knew best. When invited, they willingly responded and carried their basket-making materials, tools, basket examples, a small sack of acorns to crack, another small sack of dried acorn meats to grind into flour, a heavy grinding slab, a mano to grind the nut meats, a winnowing tray, and a *lok som* to demonstrate the leeching process to make the flour edible. Adults were amazed. Children participated with wide-eyed enthusiasm. These youngsters were Daisy and Lilly's children. After Daisy died, Lilly, as a respected Maidu elder, delivered the Maidu message alone for over three decades without any tribal help.

Their lives symbolized a humble persistence illustrating confident pride in their centuries-old culture. They understood and used their environment wisely. Earthmaker planted gray willows for them and gently told them, "Daisy, faithful one, pick my willows in the meadow. Make our baskets. Tell of everlasting beauty. Lilly, the solitary and regal mountain flower, shine brightly under the mighty pines. Deliver the Maidu message. Pick gray willows. You need bundles of them. Prepare willows. Make baskets to tell our Mountain Maidu stories." As caressing lake breezes weave through the willows over the meadow up into the mountain forests, Earthmaker whispered, "Look, Daisy and Lilly live."

Acknowledgments

Many thanks to the following people for their gracious help and encouragement through this heartfelt journey: Kit Kurtz, Roya Sabri, Tom Peek, Ken and Emi Holton, Lori Voorhees PhD, Heather Shotwell, Bruce and Nan Shelly, Teri Castaneda PhD, Lynn Smith, Eric Leseur, Georgia Bollinger, Marvin Hilpert, and Doug Tough.

Other Books by Pat Lindgren-Kurtz

The following companion books by Patricia Lindgren-Kurtz offer further information on the Mountain Maidu and the women weavers of the Meadows–Baker family.

Mountain Maidu and Pioneers, A History of Indian Valley, Plumas County, California, 1850–1920. iUniverse, 1663 Liberty Drive, Bloomington, IN 47403 (1-800-288-4677) www.iuniverse.com.

Our Precious Legacy, Mountain Maidu Baskets from the Meadows–Baker Families. A museum catalog published for the *Our Precious Legacy* exhibit opening, September 18, 2010. Maidu Museum, 1970 Johnson Ranch Road, Roseville, CA 95661 (916-774-5934) www.roseville.ca.us. indianmuseum. Phone orders and credit card payments accepted.

Suggested References

Purdy, Tim I. *The Lake Almanor Story.* Lahontan Images, Susanville, California, 2007.

Schultz, Paul E. *Indians of Lassen Volcanic National Park and Vicinity,* Loomis Museum Association, Mineral, California, 1954.

Young, Jim, *Plumas County, History of the Feather River Region, [California]* Arcadia Publishing, San Francisco, CA, 2003.